FRANCIS OF ROME
& FRANCIS OF ASSISI

FRANCIS OF ROME
& FRANCIS OF ASSISI

A New Spring in the Church

LEONARDO BOFF

Translated by Dinah Livingstone

ORBIS BOOKS
Maryknoll, New York 10545

Founded in 1970, Orbis Books endeavors to publish works that enlighten the mind, nourish the spirit, and challenge the conscience. The publishing arm of the Maryknoll Fathers and Brothers, Orbis seeks to explore the global dimensions of the Christian faith and mission, to invite dialogue with diverse cultures and religious traditions, and to serve the cause of reconciliation and peace. The books published reflect the views of their authors and do not represent the official position of the Maryknoll Society. To learn more about Maryknoll and Orbis Books, please visit our website at www.maryknollsociety.org.

Translation copyright © 2014 by Orbis Books.

Much of this work was translated from the Spanish edition of *Francisco de Roma y Francisco de Asís: ¿Una Nueva Primavera en la Iglesia?*, © 2013 by Ediciones Dabar, Mexico City. Additional material is original to this edition. In addition to Dinah Livingstone, thanks to Adam Taylor and Samantha Pinotti for help with the translation of "What Francis Is Not," and "What Francis Is."

Published by Orbis Books, Box 302, Maryknoll, NY 10545-0302.

Manufactured in the United States of America
Manuscript editing and typesetting by Joan Weber Laflamme.

Library of Congress Cataloging-in-Publication Data
Boff, Leonardo.
  [Francisco de Roma y Francisco de Asis. English]
  Francis of Rome & Francis of Assisi : a new spring in the church? / Leonardo Boff; translated by Dinah Livingstone.
    pages cm
  "Much of this work was translated from the Spanish edition of 'Francisco de Roma y Francisco de Asis : una nueva primavera en la iglesia?' 2013 by Ediciones Dabar, Mexico City. Additional material is original to this edition" — E-Cip t.p. verso.
  ISBN 978-1-62698-083-9
  1. Francis, Pope, 1936– 2. Francis, of Assisi, Saint, 1182–1226. 3. Popes—Biography. I. Title. II. Title: Francis of Rome and Francis of Assisi.
BX1378.7.B6413 2014
282.092—dc23
                                                              2014002066

Contents

Introduction

No POPE IN THE CHURCH's history has chosen the name Francis. Among other names, many have chosen Leo, Gregory, Benedict, and Pius. If we think about Saint Francis, it would have been a big contradiction for previous popes to choose the name Francis. They lived in palaces, they flaunted many honorific titles, they concentrated all religious power in their hands and, for a long while, the civil power as well; they possessed lands (the Papal States), armies, treasures, and banks. They united in their person the *Imperium* and the *Sacerdotium*.

All that was exactly what Saint Francis of Assisi didn't want for himself or for his followers. They all had to be friars (from *fratres*, meaning "brothers" in medieval Latin). They called themselves *minor* (without power), as opposed to the *major* (the nobles, the great feudal lords, and the rich merchants). Saint Francis and these friars chose to live at the bottom *(in plano subsistere)*, fraternizing with the people, the poor, and those who were socially rejected like lepers.

If a pope from the world's periphery, outside old European Christendom, surprises everyone by choosing the name Francis, it is because he wants to send a message to all by the name alone. From now on, there will be an attempt to run the papacy in a new way, stripped of titles and power symbols. The emphasis will be on a church inspired by the life and example of Francis of Assisi, that is, on poverty, simplicity, humility, kinship

1

with all, including with the natural world and our sister Mother Earth herself.

It is a bold project but necessary, because it is more in keeping with the tradition of Jesus and the demands of the gospel. Above all, it responds to the needs of a globalized world, within which the church must seek its place, humbly and non-exclusively, beside other churches, religions, and spiritual paths.

The reflections in this small book try to bring together two extraordinary figures: Francis of Assisi and Francis of Rome. Certainly, the Roman Catholic Church will never be the same again. With Pope Francis, who prefers to think of himself first and foremost as bishop of Rome, and only after that as pope, a pope who wants to preside over the other churches in charity, it is very probable that a new dynasty of popes will arise coming from the new churches of Africa, Asia, and Latin America.

Up till now these have been *mirror-churches* of the European churches, but over time they have become *source-churches*, with their own way of living the faith, in dialogue with and embodied in local cultures.

Moreover, only 24 percent of Catholics live in Europe. The rest, the great majority, live in countries of the so-called Third and Fourth Worlds. This means that today Christianity is a Third World religion, which originated in the First World. So it is quite right that a pope should come from within these great Catholic majorities.

Through the work and grace of the Spirit, who always accompanies the churches on their sometimes tortuous journey, at last a pope has arisen who comes from *the ends of the earth,* as he himself says. By the name he has chosen alone—Francis—he represents a new hope for the whole church and for the whole world.

On March 16, in the Paul VI Hall, he gave an interview to the assembled journalists. He explained the name Francis quite simply, saying:

When the number of votes was reached making me pope, the Brazilian Cardinal Claudio Hummes came up to me, kissed me and said: "Don't forget the poor." Immediately, thinking of the poor, I thought of Francis of Assisi. Then I thought about the poor and about wars. During the scrutiny when the number of votes was becoming *dangerous* for me, a name came into my heart: Francis of Assisi. Francis, the man of poverty, peace, who loves and takes care of creation, a man who gives out a sense of peace, a poor man. Oh! How I would like a church that was poor and for the poor!

That says the essential thing about his name and the mission he is taking on: to coordinate and enliven the faith and hope of hundreds of millions of Catholics. From what he has said and shown in his actions, this looks set to bring about profound changes that may take the Catholic Church into the third millennium.

Note to the reader: These reflections began in response to the pope's trip to Brazil for World Youth Day, celebrated in Rio de Janeiro in July 2013. I continued to add more reflections as his vision and message continued to unfold in new and surprising ways. Doubtless by the time this book appears, there will be ample material for future reflection. God willing.

— LEONARDO BOFF

Part I

Pope Francis

A Break with the Past to Bring in the New

The Church

From Fortress to Open House

THE WORD BREAK *(RUPTURA)* IS the most adequate to understand the novelty represented by Pope Francis. This word *break* was not welcomed by the two previous popes. They strongly emphasized the continuity of the councils and the church's official teaching.

But that insistence does not fit the facts. Indeed, Pope John XXIII's (1958–63) image of the church—open dialogue with the modern world, which gave rise to the Second Vatican Council (1962–65)—is very different from that of Pius IX (1846–78), with his condemnations of democracy and modern freedoms *(Syllabus of Errors and Quanta Cura)* and the absence of any dialogue with modernity.

Suddenly, as if by magic, Pope Francis appears on the scene of history. He comes from "the ends of the Earth," the Third World, Argentina, outside the tensions of the Roman and European church, and he inaugurates another style of being pope and being church. There are no better words to describe this than the terms *break* and *beginning anew (inauguración de lo nuevo viable).*

The church no longer feels itself to be a fortress surrounded by enemies on all sides, but, as Pope Francis has reaffirmed many times, a house with open windows and doors so that those inside (pastors and church people) can go out and meet others, especially the poor and forsaken, and so that those outside can come in without "paying at the tollbooth," as he jokingly put it. It is a church of all and for all.

In order to understand this *break* and this *newness*, it is worth saying something about the great crisis.

What Kind of Church Is in Crisis?

VARIOUS FINANCIAL SCANDALS WITHIN THE Vatican Bank and especially the criminal acts of sexual abuse of the young by priests, bishops, and even a cardinal have led to a series of enormous crises within the church.

Crises of Authority, Credibility, and Leadership in the Institutional Church

These various crises have undermined the church's authority. It has been seriously affected by its various attempts to deny, disguise, and finally cover up sexual abuse by priests. Such unethical attitudes have eroded the credibility of the institution. How can the church claim to be a "specialist in human rights" and "mother and teacher of truth and morality" if, by its deeds and omissions, it openly goes against that which it preaches?

It is also a crisis of leadership because Benedict XVI committed various errors of judgment relating to evangelicals, Muslims, Jews, women, and the spirit of Vatican II in giving concessions to the followers of the schismatic Bishop Lefebvre, such as the reintroduction of the Latin Mass and prayer for the conversion of infidel Jews, and in general, because of his obsessive attack on modernity, seen negatively as decadence and the source of all kinds of errors, especially relativism. That was obstinately condemned but oddly enough, along the same lines but from the opposite end: absolute rigorism. It is not an intelligent strategy to combat an abuse by employing another abuse that is its polar opposite.

The consequences were disastrous. Let us take as an example the German Catholic Church, considered to be very solid. Hans Küng, in *Can We Save the Catholic Church?*, points out that in 2010 alone 250,000 faithful left the church, double the number who left in 2009. This exodus is happening all over the world, especially in the United States and in Ireland, where sexual abuse cases have reached epidemic levels. In Brazil the demoralization of the Vatican institution, among other reasons, has contributed to a drastic decrease in the number of Catholics. The census of the Brazil Institute of Geography and Statistics showed that between 2000 and 2010 the Catholic percentage decreased from 73.6 percent to 64.6 percent. In the diocese of Rio, led for thirty years by an authoritarian, sometimes despotic Archbishop Cardinal Eugenio Salles, the number of Catholics reached the historically lowest level of all, only 45.8 percent.

This crisis in the hierarchical institution has brought to light the power structure and the way in which the leadership of the community of the faithful is organized. It is an absolute monarchy, with the pope, its head, having "ordinary, supreme, full, immediate and universal power" (canon 313), increased even more by his having infallibility in matters of faith and morals.

The monopoly of power and truth is in the hands of the hierarchy, with clear signs of patriarchalism, traditionalism, clericalism, and hostility toward sex and women. The church has been ruled by what Hans Küng calls "the Roman system," whose mainstay is the figure of the pope with legal, unique, and exclusive fullness of power *(plenitudo potestatis)* over the community and each of the faithful.

The increase in critical spirit, easier access to historical documents, the resistance by more lucid Catholics to accepting the highly ideologized reasons given by the institution in its determination to give itself legitimacy, invoking its divine origin and the will of its founder

Jesus, have led many to distance themselves from this type of church and become totally indifferent to it. As the widely known historian Jean Delumeau showed in his 1978 *La Peur en Occident XIVe–XVIIIe siècles* [*Fear in the West: 14th–18th Centuries*], maintaining the faithful in ignorance and the strategy of instilling fear, which played a decisive part in the conversion of whole peoples in the past, are unacceptable today and must be condemned.

The actual Christian community is divided into two bodies: the clerical body (from pope to deacon), which holds exclusive power of command over word, doctrine, and the instruments of salvation; and the body of the laity, made up of Catholic laypeople, who have no power to make decisions and must listen, obey, and carry out the rulings that come from above. This is not a caricature but a description of what actually happens and is sanctioned by canon law.

Everything for the Hierarchy, Nothing for the Laity: Witness of Two Popes

Nothing could show this theologically problematic division better than the witness of two popes: Gregory XVI (1831–46) and Pius X (1903–14). Gregory wrote: "No one can fail to recognize that the church is an unequal society, in which God has set some as rulers and others as servants; the latter are the laity, the former the clergy." Pius is even more rigid: "Only the college of pastors has the right and the authority to direct and govern; the mass of the faithful has no right, except to let themselves be governed as an obedient flock that follows its shepherd." These expressions, which are light years away from the message of Jesus, have never been contradicted and continue to keep their theoretical and practical force.

For its part, the laity has also organized itself into movements and communities (not beyond the scope of the clerical body) and well on the sidelines. These run on the principle of communion and egalitarian participation, power is rotating, duties are assigned among members according to their capacities and skills; everyone takes part, everyone has a voice and decides collectively on the way the community should go. Scripture has a central place, read and commented on in the community and applied to particular situations.

These groups are not opposed to the hierarchical papal church and are even pleased when a member of the hierarchy shares in the life of their communities. But it must be stressed that they follow a different logic—not parallel but different. However, they still suffer from the split between clergy and laity, because the majority realizes that this split does not correspond to Jesus' dream that all should be brothers and sisters and that no one should want to be called father or instructor, "for you have one Father—the one in heaven . . . for you have one instructor, the Messiah" (Mt 23:9–10). That is always denied.

Which of the two kinds of church is in crisis and openly degenerating today? It is the monarchical-absolutist church institution, whose reasoning does not convince the faithful or accord with common sense or the sense of right and justice, which has made itself felt increasingly over the last few centuries, not without Christianity's influence. This kind of church is neither progressive nor traditionalist; it is simply medieval and derives from the ideology of absolute monarchy by the will of God.

Things do not drop readymade from heaven. Neither does Jesus produce them from up his sleeve. They have been developed historically in a slow but persistent process of accumulation of power till it reaches the absolute, equal to the power of God (the pope as God's representative). Here Hobbes's astute observation is pertinent: "Power can only be guaranteed by seeking more and more power," until it attains its supreme and divine form. This is what happened with the power of the Roman popes and the Catholic hierarchy. That highly concentrated form of power was at the heart of the crisis in the past, and it has now become even more serious.

Let us spend some time considering the nub of the crisis: the concentration of sacred power in a few hands.

How the Pope Acquired Absolutist Monarchical Power

THE CONCENTRATION OF SACRED POWER is the result of a historical process. It was not so at the beginning. The church was a community of brothers and sisters. The figure of pope did not yet exist. The one who ruled the church was the emperor, not the bishop of Rome or of Constantinople, the two imperial capitals. Hence, Emperor Constantine summoned the first ecumenical council, the Council of Nicea (325), to decide the question of Christ's divinity. Even as late as the sixth century the emperor, Justinian, who reunited the two parts of the empire, West and East, claimed the right to the primacy for himself, not for the bishop of Rome. However, because the tombs of Peter and Paul were in Rome, the Roman church had special prestige. So did its bishops, who held "presidency in love" over the others and "the office of Peter," which was to strengthen in faith, not to strengthen Peter's supremacy in government.

Everything changed with Pope Leo I (440–61), a great lawyer and man of state. He copied the Roman form of government, which was the absolutism and authoritarianism of the emperor. He began to interpret the three New Testament texts referring to Peter in strictly legal terms: Peter as the rock on which the church was to be built (Mt 16:18); Peter as the strengthener of faith (Lk 22:32); and Peter as the shepherd who must look after his sheep (Jn 21:15). The biblical meaning, Jesus' meaning, goes in completely the opposite direction: love, service, and renunciation of all honor. But the reading in terms of absolutist Roman law prevailed.

Consequently, Leo I assumed the title of *supreme pontiff and pope* in its original sense. After that, the following popes began to use the imperial insignia and robes: the stoles, the pallium, the *mozzetta* (shoulder cape), they set themselves up in palaces that remain to this day for cardinals and archbishops, a fact that scandalizes many Christians who read in the Gospels that Jesus was a poor workman without posh clothes. It became clear that the members of the hierarchy were closer to Herod's palace than the Bethlehem cave.

But there is something that is difficult for us to understand: in their eagerness to legitimate and guarantee the pope's absolute power, they forged a series of false documents.

First was a so-called letter of Pope Clement (d. 96), Peter's successor in Rome, addressed to James, the brother of the Lord, the church's ruler in Jerusalem. This letter said that before he died, Peter had determined that he, Clement, should be his single legitimate successor. And, of course, those who came after him. An even greater forgery was the famous *Donation of Constantine,* a document forged in the time of Leo I, according to which Constantine had given to the pope of Rome the gift of the whole Roman Empire. Later, in disputes with the Frankish kings, there was another great forgery, the *Pseudo-Isidorean Decretals,* which gathered together false documents and letters as if they came from the early centuries, reinforcing the legal primacy of the pope of Rome. The climax was *Gratian's Decretum* in the thirteenth century, held to be the basis of canon law, but which was founded on forgeries and rules that reinforced the central power of Rome, as well as on other genuine canons that were circulating in the churches.

All this was unmasked later but without producing any change at all in the absolutism of the popes. But it is disgraceful. Adult Christians ought to be aware of the tricks used in order to maintain a power that is against tradition and the ideals of Jesus and that obscures the attractive Christian message of a new way of exercising power—serving and sharing.

Subsequently, there was a crescendo of papal power: In his *Dictatus Papae* [the dictatorship of the pope] Gregory VII (d. 1085) proclaimed himself absolute lord of the church and the world; Innocent III (d. 1216) announced himself as the vicar-representative of Christ; and finally, Innocent IV (d. 1254) raised himself to become God's representative. Eventually, under Pius IX in 1870, the pope was proclaimed infallible in the area of doctrine and morals.

Oddly enough, all of these excesses have never been denounced or corrected by the hierarchical church because the hierarchy benefits from them. They continue to be a scandal for those who believe in the poor Nazarene, the humble Mediterranean artisan and peasant, who was persecuted, executed on the cross, and rose again to rise up against all those seeking power and yet more power, even within the church. This hierarchical view of the papacy is guilty of an unforgivable oversight: according to Jesus' gospel (Mt 25:45), the true vicar-representatives of Christ are the poor, the hungry, and the thirsty. The hierarchy exists to serve them, not to displace them. When the time comes, they, the poor, will be our judges.

Given the scandals that have occurred within the church, a historico-critical reflection is necessary, to look beyond the drama, so that the faithful can live by a critical and adult faith.

The Church Institution
as *Casta Meretrix*—Chaste Prostitute

ANYONE WHO KNOWS SOME CHURCH history—and we professionals in this area have to study it in detail—is not surprised by the crimes of sexual abuse committed by clergy and the financial crimes of the Vatican Bank, which have been broadcast throughout the media.

In the institutional church's two-thousand-year history, there have been catastrophic moments in the papacy, with popes who were adulterers, murderers, and traffickers. According to the great historian Cardinal Baronio, from Pope Formosus (891–96) to Pope Sylvester (999–1003), there was the "pornocratic era" of the church's top hierarchy. Few popes escaped being overthrown or murdered. Sergius III (904–11), for example, is rumored to have murdered his two predecessors, the antipope Christopher and Leo V.

The great transformation of the church as a whole happened under Pope Gregory VII in the year 1077, with consequences for all its later history. The great historian of ecclesiological ideas, Dominican Yves Congar, considered this date to be the greatest revolution there has ever been in the church. From a church-community it became a monarchical and absolutist institution-society, organized as a pyramid, as it continues to this day.

Indeed, canon 331 of present Canon Law adopts this understanding, attributing to the pope powers that really belong to no mortal but to God alone: "In virtue of his office, the Pope holds ordinary, supreme, full, immediate and universal power," which in some specific cases is "infallible."

It is always said that the church is "saint and sinner" and must be "always reformed." But this is not what happened over centuries, or even after the explicit desire expressed at Vatican II and by the two last popes. As the oldest institution in the West, the Roman Catholic Church incorporated privileges, habits, palatial and princely political customs, and tactics of resistance and opposition that in practice have thwarted all attempts at reform.

But under Pope Benedict XVI, a situation that even included criminal practices led to such a state of utter demoralization that reform became a matter of extreme urgency. Otherwise, the institution, sadly aged and in its twilight years, would weaken and die. The current scandals have always existed in the Vatican curia, but there were no providential "Vati-leaks" to make them public and outrage the pope and the majority of Christians.

These evils in the sacred space and focal point for the whole of Christianity—the papacy (where virtue and holiness should shine)—are a consequence of that absolutist centralization of papal power. This makes everyone vassals, subservient, hungry to be physically close to the bearer of supreme power, the pope. By its nature absolute power limits and even denies the freedom of others. It encourages the creation of anti-power groups, cliques of bureaucrats of the sacred, one against another. It widely practices simony, which means buying and selling favors; it promotes adulation and destroys the mechanisms of transparency. At bottom, everybody distrusts everybody else. And each looks out for his own personal satisfaction as best he can. That is why the observance of celibacy has always been a problem within the Vatican curia, as we are seeing now with the alleged existence of an active gay prostitution network.

For as long as this power does not decentralize and give all sectors of the people of God, both men and women, a greater share in the management of the church's affairs, the tumor, which Pope Francis called "leprosy," will remain. From the time of the Reformation we have heard the cry: "Reform of head and members." As this did not happen, the Reformation arose as a desperate bid by the reformers to bring it about of their own accord.

For the information of Christians and those interested in church affairs, let us return to the question of the scandals. As we said earlier, the intention is to look beyond the drama in order to gain a less idealistic and sometimes even idolatrous notion of the hierarchy and the figure of the pope and to free us for the freedom to which Christ has called us (Gal 5:1). This discussion of the scandals is not for the pleasure of being negative or a desire to add demoralization upon demoralization. Christians must be grown up. They must not let themselves be treated as infants or allow themselves to be denied knowledge of theology and history in order to see how human, sometimes all too human, the institution that comes to us from the apostles can be.

There is a long theological tradition that refers to the church as *casta meretrix* (chaste prostitute). This was discussed in detail by a great theologian Hans Urs von Balthasar (*Sponsa Verbi*, Einsiedeln, 1971, 203–305). On various occasions theologian Joseph Ratzinger, later Pope Benedict XVI, also referred to this term. The church is a *meretrix* that engages every night in prostitution; it is *casta* because Christ takes pity on it every morning, washes it and loves it.

The *habitus meretrius* of the institution—the vice of prostitution or harlotry—was fiercely criticized by the fathers of the church like Saint Ambrose, Saint Augustine, Saint Jerome, and others. Saint Peter Damian even called Gregory VII, mentioned above, "Saint Satan" (D. Romag, *Compendio de la historia de la Iglesia*, vol. 2, Petropolis, 112). That bad name reminds us of what Christ called Peter. Because of his profession of faith, he calls him "rock," but because of his little faith and failure to understand God's plan he calls him "Satan" (Mt 16: 23). Saint Paul sounds like a modern man talking when he says furiously of his opponents: "I wish those who unsettle you would castrate themselves" (Gal 5:12).

So there is a space for prophecy in the church and for the denunciation of irregularities that can occur within the church and also among the faithful.

Let us mention another example taken from a saint who is loved by most Catholics for his candor and kindness: Saint Anthony of Padua. In his sermons, which were famous at the time, he is not at all sweet or soft. He strongly criticizes the extravagant prelates of his time. He says: "They are most impudent dogs, having a harlot's forehead, refusing to blush" (I am using the critical Latin edition published in Lisbon, 2 vols., 1895). This was the sermon for the fourth Sunday after Pentecost (1:278). On another occasion he calls bishops "apes on the roof, presiding from there over the people of God" (1:348), and he continues: "The bishop of the church is a slave who claims to reign, a wicked prince, a roaring lion, a bear hungry for prey, who robs the poor" (1:348). Finally on the feast of Saint Peter, he raises his voice and denounces them: "Note that Christ said 'feed' three times, but not once 'shear' or 'milk.' . . . Woe to the man who does not feed even once, but shears and milks three or four times. . . . He is like Dagon before the ark of the Lord [1 Kg(Sm) 5:2]. He keeps the image, not the reality" (2:918).

Theologian Joseph Ratzinger explains the meaning of this kind of prophetic denunciation: "The meaning of the prophecy really lies less in certain predictions than in prophetic protest: protest against the self-satisfaction of institutions, who go for ritual instead of morality and ceremonies instead of conversion" (*Das neue Volk Gottes*, Düsseldorf, 1969).

In his criticism Ratzinger stresses the split we mentioned in the figure of Peter: before Easter he was the traitor, and after Pentecost the faithful follower. Peter continues living with this tension of before and after. He continues to be two things: a rock and a scandal. Ratzinger adds: "And hasn't this been a constant phenomenon throughout the whole history of the church, that the pope, Peter's successor, has been both *petra* and *skandalon*, God's rock and a stumbling stone?'

Where do we want to get to with all of this? We want to come to a recognition that the church, as an institution of popes, bishops, and priests, is composed of men who can betray, deny, and make religious power a matter of business or an instrument of self-satisfaction. Recognizing this is therapeutic because it cures us of an idolatrous ideology toward the figure of the pope, who is regarded as practically infallible. That attitude is visible in conservative and fundamentalist Catholic lay movements and also in groups of priests. In some there exists a real *papolatry*, which the popes have always condemned.

The present crisis led to the resignation of Pope Benedict XVI, who realized that he no longer had the necessary strength to heal such grave scandals. He "threw in the towel" with humility and great serenity. Let someone younger come and take on the arduous task of cleaning up the corruption in the Vatican curia and the world of sexual abuse. Let him sanction, dismiss, and send the most obstinate to a convent to do penance and amend their lives. And divine Providence has sent us Pope Francis.

Only someone who loves the church can make the criticisms we have made, citing texts from classical authorities of the past. Anyone who has stopped loving someone becomes indifferent to that person's—or institution's—life and destiny.

We do not want Christians to cultivate feelings of abandonment and indifference. However bad its historical errors and mistakes have been, the church institution keeps the sacred memory of Jesus and the grammar of the Gospels. The church preaches liberation, knowing that the church itself does not free people; others do that.

So it is worth staying in the church, as did Saint Francis, Dom Helder Camara, John XXIII, and the notable theologians who helped make the Second Vatican Council, and theologians like de Lubac, Chenu, Rahner, and others, who had all been condemned beforehand by the so-called Holy Office. We must help the church rid itself of this shame by fostering Jesus' dream of a reign of justice and reconciliation with God and by following his cause and destiny, rather than by mere justified indignation, which on its own can easily become phariseeism and moralism.

Can We Save the Catholic Church?

THIS QUESTION WAS ASKED BY one of the most famous and fertile theologians in the Catholic area, Swiss German Hans Küng, in one of his books that bears the same title (2013; German original *Ist die Kirche noch zu retten?* [2011]).

Küng is known worldwide for the enthusiastic way in which he fostered the renewal of the church, together with his colleague in the University of Tübingen, Josph Ratzinger. He has written an enormous amount on the church, ecumenism, religions, world ethics, and other relevant topics. He was severely penalized by the Congregation for the Doctrine of the Faith (successor to the Inquisition) for a book that questioned papal infallibility. He did not leave the church but devoted himself as few others have done to its reform with books, open letters, and calls to bishops and the Christian community to open a dialogue with the modern world and with the new planetary situation of humanity.

People who are sons and daughters of our time cannot be evangelized by presenting them with a model of the church as a bastion of conservatism and authoritarianism, a church that sees itself as a fortress besieged by modernity that it holds responsible for relativism of every sort. That was the vision of the last two popes, John Paul II and Benedict XVI: no to reforms and a return to tradition and strict discipline, orchestrated by the ecclesiastical hierarchy.

Can We Save the Catholic Church? is an almost desperate cry for changes, and at the same time, a generous manifestation of hope that these are possible and necessary, if the church is not to suffer a disastrous institutional collapse.

First of all, it is clear that when Küng and I speak of the church, we mean the community of those who are committed to the figure, the tradition, and the cause of Jesus, whose focus is unconditional love, the centrality of the poor and invisible, the communion of all human beings, and the revelation that we are sons and daughters of God. Jesus himself implied that he was God's own son who took our contradictory humanity upon himself. This is the original and true meaning of church. But historically the word *church* has been appropriated by the hierarchy (from pope to priests); it identifies and presents itself alone as church. But we must always distinguish between church as the universal community of the faithful and the hierarchy, which is its leading and inspiring body.

What is in deep crisis is the latter, the idea of church as hierarchy, which Küng calls the "Roman system" or "the institutional-hierarchical church" or "the monarchical-absolutist structure of command," whose seat is in the Vatican and whose center is the figure of the pope with the apparatus surrounding him: the Roman curia. This crisis has been going on for centuries, and the cry for change echoes throughout the history of the church, culminating in the sixteenth-century Reformation and in the Second Vatican Council (1962–65) of our own time. In structural terms the reforms were always superficial or postponed or simply aborted.

However, in recent times the crisis has become desperately serious. The church institution (pope, cardinals, bishops, and priests), I repeat, not the great community of the faithful, has been struck in its heart in what was its great claim: to be a "guide and teacher of morals" for all humanity. Some well-known facts have put that claim into check and have discredited the church institution, which has caused many of the faithful to leave.

The financial scandals involving the Vatican Bank, which became a sort of off-shore money-laundering outfit; the secret documents stolen, perhaps even from the pope's table by his own secretary, and sold to newspapers, revealing the power intrigues between cardinals; and especially the question of sexual abuse by priests, thousands of cases in different countries, most visibly in the United States, which involve, priests, bishops, and even the cardinal of Vienna, Hans Hermann Groer. There was the very seriously wrong instruction given by the then-Cardinal Ratzinger to all the bishops of the world to cover up, under pontifical seal, the sexual abuses of minors to prevent abusers from being denounced to the civil authorities. In the end the pope had to recognize the criminal character of sexual abuse and accept that it should be tried by the civil courts.

With his irrefutable historical erudition, Küng shows the steps taken by the popes to move from being Peter's successors to vicars of Christ and representatives of God on earth. The titles that canon 331 confers upon the pope are so high that in reality they belong to God alone. An absolute papal monarchy with a golden crosier does not accord with the wooden crook of the good shepherd who lovingly cares for his sheep and strengthens them in the faith, as the Master demanded (Lk 22:32). Pope Francis has gotten rid of all these symbols and returned to the simplicity and ideal of poverty of his patron, Saint Francis of Assisi.

But the church can be saved as long as it is inspired by the tradition of Jesus, returns to drink from the well of the gospel, sets out to serve the world rather than itself, and puts the poor at the center in a quest for liberation and social justice. Then it is good not only for Christians but for the whole world. It is a force for humanization and peace among peoples.

Two Models of a Church in Tension

THE PROFILE OF EACH POPE depends a lot on the way in which he deals with the internal tensions of the church, especially on how he balances two models of church in tension. Basically, the central question is this: what is the position and mission of the church in the world?

To answer this big question we have to understand the two pillars on which the church rests and is built: the kingdom and the world.

The *kingdom* is the central message of Jesus, his utopia of a complete revolution that reconciles creation with itself and with God.

The *world* is the place where the church carries out its service to the kingdom and where it builds itself.

If we think the church is too closely bound to the kingdom, we run the risk of spiritualization and idealism. If it is too close to the world, there is the temptation of worldliness and politicization. The important thing is to know how to articulate kingdom-world-church. It belongs to the kingdom and also to the world. It has a historical dimension, with all its contradictions, and another, transcendent dimension.

How should the church live with this tension in the world and in history? We have two different models, in tension and sometimes in conflict: the church of *witness* and the church of *dialogue.*

The model of *witness* states the following with conviction: we have the deposit of faith, which contains all the truths necessary for salvation; we have the sacraments, which communicate grace; we have a well-defined morality; we have the certainty that the Catholic Church is the church of Christ, the only true church; we have the pope who enjoys infallibility in questions of faith and morals; we have a hierarchy that governs the faithful people; and we have the promise of permanent help from the Holy Spirit. It witnesses all this to the world, which will never achieve salvation on its own. The world must pass through the mediation of the church, without which there is no salvation.

Christians following this model feel they are imbued with a unique saving mission. They are fundamentalist and little given to dialogue. Why dialogue? We already have it all. Dialogue is only to facilitate conversion. As can be seen, this is an attitude with a conservative, inward-looking tendency.

The *dialogue* model starts from other assumptions: the kingdom is greater than the church and also finds secular fulfillment wherever there is truth, love, and justice; the risen Christ has cosmic dimensions and is pushing evolution toward a good end; the Spirit is always present in history and in good people, arriving before the missionary because it was already among peoples in the form of solidarity, love, and compassion. God never abandons his own, and offers to all the opportunity of salvation, because he produced them from his heart so that one day they might live happily in the kingdom of the freed. The church's mission is to be a sign of this history of God within human history and also an instrument for its implementation, together with other spiritual paths. If both religious and reality secular reality are impregnated with God, we must all enter into dialogue: exchange, learn from one another, and make the human journey toward the promised happiness easier and safer. This is the attitude of progressive Christians who are open to dialogue with the whole world.

The first model of *witness* is that of the traditional church, which promoted the missions in Asia, Africa, and

Latin America, and was even complicit in the destruction and domination of thousands of indigenous, African, and Asian peoples. It was the model of Pope John Paul II, who traveled the world brandishing the cross as a testimony that salvation came from it. It was the even more radicalized model of Benedict XVI, who denied the name of church to the evangelical churches and seriously offended them; he directly attacked modernity because he saw it negatively as relativist and secularist. Although he did not deny it all value, he saw the Christian faith as the source of that value. He reduced the church to an isolated island or fortress surrounded by enemies on every side from whom it had to defend itself.

The *dialogue* model is that of Vatican II and of Medellín and Puebla in Latin America, and clearly, of Pope Francis. They see Christianity not as a deposit, a closed system that risks becoming fossilized, but as a spring of clear, living waters that can be channeled by many cultural conduits, a place of mutual apprenticeship, because we are all bearers of the Creator Spirit and the essence of Jesus' dream.

The first model, that of *witness,* made many Christians feel devalued in their professional knowledge; they no longer felt the church to be their spiritual home, and disconsolately, they moved away from the church but not from Christian values and the generous utopia of Jesus.

The second model, of *dialogue,* brought many together, because they felt at home, helping to build an apprentice-church that was open to dialogue with all. The effect was a feeling of freedom and creativity. This made it worthwhile to be a Christian. This is the Francis effect that is happening in all parts of the church.

The *dialogue* model is urgently necessary if the church wants to emerge from the crisis it is in, which has wounded it to the heart of its honor, both morally and spiritually.

We must discern intelligently what will best serve the Christian message now in the context of a social and ecological crisis with dire consequences. The central problem is not the church but the future of Mother Earth, of life, and of our civilization. How can the church help with this? Only by taking part in dialogue and joining forces with others. As we shall see, Pope France sets himself decisively on this road of dialogue and humble service to all humanity.

What Kind of Church Do We Want, and Does Such a Church Have a Future?

AT THE END OF OUR reflections in Part I a question arises: what sort of church do we want, and does such a church have a future in view of the new phase of humanity we are in, the planetary phase? It is the church that remains faithful to the tradition of Jesus and the apostles and is not afraid to become embodied in the world and in different cultures in order to bring Jesus' liberating message to all.

The heart of Jesus' preaching was not the church but the kingdom of God: a utopia of total revolution/ reconciliation for all creation. This is so certain that the Gospels, with the exception of Matthew, never speak of *church* but always of *kingdom*. With the rejection of Jesus' person and message, the kingdom did not come, and the church arose as the community of those bearing witness to Jesus' resurrection and keeping his legacy with the intention of living it out in history.

From the beginning there was a split. The main body of Christians took up Christianity as a spiritual path, in dialogue with the surrounding culture. Another, much smaller group, agreed to take on, under the emperor's control, the moral leadership of the Roman Empire, which was in a state of decadence. This group copied the imperial legal-political structures for the organization of the faith community. The hierarchy structured itself around the category of sacred power (*sacra potestas*). This was a high-risk strategy, because if there was one thing Christ always rejected, it was power. For him, when power in its three expressions, as they appear in the temptations in the wilderness—the prophetic, the religious, and the political—becomes not service but domination, it belongs to the diabolical sphere. Nevertheless, that was the path followed by the hierarchical church-institution in the form of an absolutist monarchy, which refuses the laity, the great majority of the faithful, any share in this power. That has persisted up to our own time in the context of a very serious crisis of confidence.

What happens is that when power rules, love disappears. Indeed, the organizational style of the hierarchical church is bureaucratic, formal, and at times inflexible. In it everything has to be paid for; nothing ever is forgotten or forgiven. There is practically no space for compassion, for any real understanding of the divorced and homosexuals, for example. There is the imposition of celibacy upon priests, the deep-rooted anti-feminism, the distrust of anything to do with sexuality and pleasure, the personality cult of the pope, the claim to be the only true church and the "only guardian established by God of the eternal, universal, and unchangeable natural law," which then, in the words of Benedict XVI, "assumes a guiding function over the whole of humanity." Even in the year 2000 then-Cardinal Ratzinger repeated in the document *Dominus Iesus* the medieval doctrine that there is "no salvation outside the church" and those outside it "run a grave risk of being lost." Certainly that kind of church cannot be saved. It is slowly losing sustainability throughout the whole world.

So what sort of church can have a future? A church that is humbly inspired by the tradition of Jesus and the apostles, that is to say, one that returns to the figure of the historical Jesus, a simple and prophetic workman, incarnate Son, with a divine mission to announce that God, a good Father, is there with grace and mercy for all; a church that recognizes other churches as different expressions of the sacred legacy of Jesus; a church open to dialogue with all other religions and spiritual paths, seeing in them the action of the Spirit, who always arrives before the missionary; a church that is prepared to learn from all humanity's accumulated wisdom; a church that renounces all power and will not make a spectacle of the faith so that it becomes a mere facade of a nonexistent vitality; a church that presents itself as advocate and defender of the oppressed in any class, and is prepared to suffer persecution and martyrdom like its founder; a church in which the pope has the courage to renounce the claim to legal power over all and becomes a sign of unity and focus for the Christian project with its pastoral mission to strengthen all in faith, hope, and love.

This church is within the bounds of possibility. All that is needed is to run our lives in accordance with the ideals of the tradition of Jesus and to fill ourselves with the spirit of the gospel. Then the church would really become a church of human beings, of Jesus, of God—the proof that Jesus' utopia of the kingdom is true. It would become a space to bring about of the kingdom of the freed, to which we are all summoned.

Part II

Francis of Rome
and Francis of Assisi

A New Spring in the Church

Two Named Francis

Francis of Assisi and Francis of Rome, Called to Restore the Church

IT WAS PROVIDENTIAL THAT WHEN Argentine Cardinal Jorge Mario Bergoglio was elected pope, he chose the name Francis. For both Francis of Assisi and Francis of Rome had a mission, each in his own time: to restore Christ's church.

Saint Francis felt the call to rescue the gospel meaning of the church—almost lost during the period of imperial power of the popes—from the pomp of palaces for cardinals and bishops and the general decadence that abounded everywhere.

Francis began his conversion when he heard the crucifix in the small church of San Damiano saying to him: "Francis, go and restore my house, because it is in ruins."

Francis took these words literally and rebuilt the church of Porciúncula, which was in ruins. It still stands in Assisi inside a huge cathedral. Later, he realized that the message meant something spiritual: to restore the *church that Christ had redeemed with his blood.* And he began his movement to renew the church, which was ruled by the most powerful pope in history, Innocent III.

He began by living with lepers. Arm in arm with one of them he walked the roads preaching the gospel of simplicity in the vernacular language, not in Latin.

It is good to know that Francis was never a priest, but just a simple layman. Only at the end of his life, when the popes forbade laypeople to preach, did he agree to be made a deacon, on condition that he received no pay for the job.

Why did Cardinal Jorge Mario Bergoglio choose the name Francis? It was for exactly the same reasons that made the young man recently converted to the gospel, Francis of Assisi, become the pioneer of a movement to restore the medieval church.

Like many others, Pope Francis has also realized that the present-day church is in a state of ruin because of the demoralization caused by various financial and moral scandals committed by priests, bishops, and even cardinals, which sully what was most precious for the church: its morality and credibility.

Francis is not only a name; it is a project to create a church that is poor, simple, evangelical, and stripped of all trappings. Francis began a church that walked the roads together with the most lowly; he created the first communities of brothers who prayed the breviary under trees with the birds. It was an ecological church that called all creatures by the beautiful name of *brothers and sisters*.

That is the church model also inspiring Francis of Rome: *a poor church for the poor*, as he put it very well himself, a church that tries to be faithful to the legacy of Jesus. Its pastors must *smell of sheep*, as he humorously expressed it in a homily to priests in Rome. That means they should walk side by side with the people.

As pope, he himself knows this and said it plainly: he must guide the faithful, but he must also walk among them, sharing the journey, listening to the people, welcoming their wisdom, and feeling part of the people of God.

Francis of Assisi was obedient to the church of the popes, and at the same time he went his own way with the gospel of poverty in his hand and heart. In 1970, Joseph Ratzinger (later Pope Benedict XVI) wrote: "Francis's no to that type of church [powerful and rich] could not be more radical; it is what we would call prophetic protest" (*Zeit Jesu*, Freiburg-Vienna, 269). It does not attack or criticize the dominant style; rather, it simply inaugurates and enacts a new style.

I believe Pope Francis is thinking of a church of community, away from palaces and power symbols. That is why he did not want to live in the papal apartment in the Apostolic Palace but in Saint Martha's guesthouse, sharing the table with fellow residents.

In his first public appearance after he was elected pope, he demonstrated a new way of being. Normally popes wear a cape on their shoulders, the *mozzetta*, made of silk in summer and velvet and ermine in winter; previously the *mozzetta* could be worn only by the emperors. Pope Francis appears dressed simply in white, with the iron cross he wore as bishop and afterward as cardinal of Buenos Aires.

Here we highlight three points in his first words, which have great symbolic significance.

First: He has said he wants to preside in charity. This is a common expression since the Reformation and is used by the best theologians of ecumenism. The pope must not preside as an absolute monarch, clothed in sacred power as canon law prescribes (canon 331). According to Jesus, he must preside in love and strengthen the faith of his brothers and sisters.

Second: He has put the people of God at the center. This idea, emphasized so strongly at the Second Vatican Council, was minimized by the two popes preceding him, who were inclined toward a hierarchical and clerical church. Pope Francis humbly asks the people of God to pray for him and bless him. Only then will he bless the people of God. That means he is here to serve and not to be served. He asks the people to help him on the journey together. And he begs for fellowship with all humanity, because human beings do not treat one another as brothers and sisters; they are in thrall to the mechanisms of the neo-liberal economy that makes so many human beings superfluous and unemployed.

Third: He has shunned all papal ostentation. He did not spread wide his arms in a showy gesture to greet the people. He stood still, serious and quiet, and I would even venture to say, looking rather scared. His white figure could barely be seen as he looked kindly at the crowd, beaming with peace and trust. He used humor, speaking without "official-ese," like a pastor to his flock. He ended by wishing them all *good night and sleep well.*

We should stress that this is a pope who comes from the South, where the poor are to be found and where 60 percent of Catholics live. With his experience as a pastor, with a new vision of things "from below," he will be able to reform the curia, decentralize the administration, and give the church a different and credible face.

That is the great hope of all who follow the church's journey in the world. And surely we will not be disappointed, because he has Francis of Assisi as his patron and inspiration. And that figure of Francis makes many moral and spiritual demands.

Francis of Assisi and Francis of Rome

What Have They in Common?

Since he took the name Francis when he was elected bishop of Rome and therefore pope, there will inevitably be comparisons between the two: Francis of Assisi and Francis of Rome. Moreover, Francis of Rome referred explicitly to Francis of Assisi. Of course, we cannot just make a straight comparison between the two, but we can find common points of inspiration, which could change the face of the church to become more in the spirit of Saint Francis, who was simple, humble, and poor.

There is one undeniable point in common: the crisis in the church as an institution. Young Francis of Assisi says he heard a voice coming from the crucifix in San Damiano saying: "Francis, go and restore my house, because it is in ruins." Giotto represents him well, shouldering the heavy church building, which is falling down.

At present we are also experiencing a serious crisis because of the internal scandals in the church institution. The universal cry has been heard (the voice of the people is the voice of God): "Repair the church, which is in ruins in its morality and in its credibility." It was then that a cardinal, Jorge Mario Bergoglio of Buenos Aires, "coming from the ends of the earth," as he himself said, was given the mission to restore the church, now as pope, inspired by Francis of Assisi.

In Saint Francis's time, Pope Innocent III reigned (1198–1216), calling himself Christ's representative. With him, the highest level of secularization of the church institution was reached, with explicit intentions of *dominium mundi*—to rule the world. Indeed, for a brief period practically the whole of Europe, even Russia, was subject to the pope. He lived in great pomp and glory. In 1209, assailed by many doubts, Innocent III recognized Francis of Assisi's way of poverty. The crisis was theological. A temporal and sacred empire-church was not in accord with what Jesus wanted: power as service and the last coming first.

Francis was the living antithesis of the imperial church. To the gospel of power he presented the power of the gospel, read and accepted literally; to the wealth of the popes, bishops, and abbots, he proposed total renunciation, radical poverty, and extreme simplicity; for those who command and stand out above the rest, he postulated the humility of the powerless, who are at rock bottom. He did not have any place in the clerical or monastic structure but was a layman who spent barely three interrupted years in school and wrote Latin badly. He was led by the gospel and lived by it without sophisticated interpretations, on the outskirts of cities where the poor and lepers are, and in the midst of nature, experiencing a cosmic brotherhood with all creatures.

From the periphery he spoke to the center, pleading for conversion. Without making any explicit criticism, he began a great reform "from below" but did not break with Rome. We are faced with an attractively human Christian genius of fascinating tenderness and exquisite care, and who exhibited the best of our humanity.

I think this strategy must have impressed Francis of Rome. The curia and the habits of the whole church need to be reformed. But it is necessary to do so without ruptures that might lacerate the body of the church.

Another point that certainly inspired Francis of Rome is the centrality that Francis of Assisi gave to the poor. He did not organize any works *for* the poor, but he lived *with* the poor and *like* the poor. Since we have known him, Francis of Rome has kept repeating that the problem of the poor cannot be resolved without the participation of the poor, it cannot be resolved by practicing philanthropy but by social justice. This will decrease the inequalities that plague Latin America and the whole world.

Another point of inspiration is very relevant today: how we should relate to Mother Earth and to scarce goods and services. In his inaugural speech at his enthronement, Francis of Rome used the word *care* more than eight times. The ethics of caring is what will save human lives and guarantee the health of ecosystems. Francis of Assisi, patron of ecology, will be the paradigm for a respectful kinship with all creatures, not from above but on the ground where every creature stands, especially those most threatened with extinction.

Francis of Assisi had a friendly relationship of real love with Clare. He praised women and the virtues, which he called "ladies." Let us hope that he may inspire Francis of Rome to cultivate a relationship with women, who are the majority in the church, not only of respect but of valuing their decision-making initiatives on how faith and spirituality should be in the new millennium. There are many people who say that the twenty-first century will be the women's century. Life is threatened, and they who generate life will know how to take care of all life forms and of our sister Mother Earth herself, as Saint Francis called her. She is alive, she is Pacha Mama, she is Gaia, she is the Great Mother who generously gives us everything we need to live. Pope Francis will need to strengthen this mission entrusted to women and to all of us.

Finally, according to philosopher Max Scheler, Francis of Assisi is the Western prototype of emotional reason, the heart's reason. This is what makes us feel for what men and women suffer, the cries of the earth, of tortured animals, smashed forests, and all who cry for protection in order to survive.

If Pope Benedict XVI, as an eminent theologian, expressed intellectual reason, Pope Francis represents the heart's intelligence, which loves people, embraces people, kisses children, and looks lovingly upon crowds.

If modern reason cannot combine with the heart's reason, we will find it difficult to take care of our common household with its disinherited sons and daughters; we will find it difficult and to foster the Franciscan conviction that a bond of kinship links all creatures together.

When we lovingly embrace the world, we are embracing God.

The Spirit of Saint Francis, an Inspiration for Pope Francis

BECAUSE THE NEW POPE CHOSE the name Francis, many have become interested in this strange figure, who was perhaps one of the most luminous that Christianity or the West itself has produced: Francis of Assisi. There are some who call him *the last Christian* or *the first since the only one, that is, Jesus Christ.*

We can be sure that when Cardinal Bergoglio chose this name, he wanted to signal a project for the church in accord with the spirit of Saint Francis, who was opposed to the church project of his time. That was expressed through temporal power over nearly the whole of Europe as far as Russia, by huge cathedrals, sumptuous palaces, and grandiose abbeys. Saint Francis opted to live by the gospel alone, literally, in the most radical poverty, with an almost naive simplicity, with a humility that drew him close to the earth, to the level of those who were the most despised in society. He lived among lepers, eating with them from the same bowl.

He never criticized the power or Rome. He simply did not follow its example. For that type of church and society, he explicitly confessed: "I want to be a *novellus pazzus*, a new madman: mad for the poor Christ and *Lady Poverty*," a poverty that gave him total freedom: being nothing, having nothing, capable of nothing, claiming nothing. The phrase is attributed to him: "I want little and the little I want is little." In fact, it was nothing. He stripped himself of every title. He thought of himself as "idiot, paltry, miserable, and vile."

With great difficulty he pursued this spiritual path, because as more and more followers joined him, he faced more opposition. They demanded that he should have convents, rules, and studying. He resisted as much as he could, but in the end he had to surrender to the mediocrity and logic of institutions, so prone to rules, order, and power. But he did not give up his dream. Frustrated, he returned to serve the lepers, allowing his movement, against his will, to become the Order of Friars Minor.

Boundless humility and radical poverty gave him the experience that comes out to meet our question: Is it possible to restore such universal fellowship that includes everyone, as he did: the sultan of Egypt whom he met on the crusade, the band of highwaymen, the fierce wolf of Gubbio, and even death itself?

With simplicity and passion Francis showed that this was possible by what he did in his life. Because he possessed nothing, he maintained a direct relationship of common life and not of possession with every creature. Because he was radically humble, he set himself on the same ground (*humus*, "humility") and beside every creature, considering all to be his brothers and sisters. He felt he was a brother to water, fire, the lark, a cloud, the sun, and everyone he met. He inaugurated a brotherhood without limits: *downward* to the very least; *sideways* with others like himself, independent of whether they were popes or laborers; *upward* with the sun, the moon, and the stars. All are brothers and sisters, children of the same Father of goodness.

Poverty and humility practiced in this way knows nothing of hypocrisy. They require limitless respect for every creature. Devotedly, he moves the worm away from the road so that he will not tread on it, bandages a broken twig so that it can heal, feeds the bees in winter when they fly astray. He stands among creatures with deep humility, feeling that he is their brother. He fraternizes with our sister Mother Earth. He does not deny the earth and the obscure roots from which we all come. By renouncing ownership of any goods, rejecting anything that could set him above other people and things in order to possess them, he emerges as the brother of all. Empty-handed and pure in heart, he goes out to meet others, offering them only courtesy, friendship, and disinterested love, full of trust and tenderness.

Universal kinship arises when we set ourselves with great humility within the bosom of creation, respecting all life forms and every creature. This cosmic fellowship, based on limitless respect, is the necessary condition for human fellowship. Without that respect and that fellowship, it will be difficult for the Declaration of Human Rights to be effective. There will always be violations for ethnic reasons, or reasons of gender, religion, or something else.

Francis's cosmic kinship, seriously adopted, can encourage our ecological concern to safeguard every species, every animal, every plant, because they are our brothers and sisters. Without real kinship we will never succeed in making the human family inhabit our sister Mother Earth with respect and care.

Such kinship requires limitless patience and also holds a promise: it can be done. We are not condemned to let the cruel beast in us take over, as it did in criminal presidents such as Videla in Argentina and Pinochet in Chile, or Chief of Police Sérgio Paranhas Fleury, a torturer in Brazil, and so many other murderers worldwide.

Let us hope that in doing his job as local and universal pastor, Francis of Rome may honor the name of Francis and show the importance today of the values embodied by the Brother and Little Poor Man of Assisi. He is a living source of inspiration, of humanitarian and profoundly ecological behavior. This is the urgent need of our time to which Pope Francis will know how to respond with simplicity and skill.

The Pope Who Pays His Bills

PEOPLE ARE NOT CONVINCED BY sermons but by deeds. Sermons can give us ideas, but it is examples that everyone grasps immediately that attract us and set us going. Many explanations confuse rather than enlighten us, whereas works speak for themselves.

The new pope, Francis, comes from outside the framework of old European Christendom, so bogged down with traditions, palaces, princely spectacles, and internal power disputes. He is distinguished by simple, down-to-earth, obvious gestures that value life's common sense. Francis is breaking all the protocols and showing that power is always a mask, even when this power is supposed to be of divine origin.

Pope Francis simply obeys the command of Jesus, who said clearly that the great ones of this world tyrannize and lord it over people. "But it is not so among you; but whoever wishes to become great among you must be your servant, and whoever wishes to be first among you must be slave of all. For the Son of Man came not to be served but to serve" (Mk 10:43–45). If Jesus said this, how can the pope, who is the bearer of his message, do otherwise?

In fact, with the establishment of the Vatican State and the absolute monarchy of popes, especially since the second millennium, the ecclesiastical institution inherited the symbols of Roman power and of the feudal nobility: brilliant clothes (like cardinals' robes), finery, gold and silver crosses and rings, and palatial habits. In the great religious houses of the Middle Ages they lived in spacious mansions.

I remember when I was a student in the room where I was lodged in the Franciscan convent in Munich, which went back to the time of William of Ockham (fourteenth century). Just one Renaissance painting on the wall was worth thousands of euros. How can we reconcile the poverty of Jesus, who had nowhere to lay his head, with the miters, the golden crosiers, the princely stoles and vestments of prelates today? The people, who are not ignorant but acute observes, see the contradiction. Such an outfit has nothing to do with the tradition of Jesus and the apostles.

According to some newspapers, when the secretary of the conclave wanted to put the *mozzetta*, the richly decorated cape, symbol of papal power, on Francis's shoulders, he responded simply: "The carnival is over. Keep this garment." And he appeared in his simple white cassock.

For me, the simplest, most transparent, and down-to-earth action by Pope Francis was that he went to the little hotel where he had been living (he never stayed in the great central house of the Jesuits in Rome) and paid his bill: ninety euros a day. He collected his things himself, packed his small suitcase, said goodbye to the workers, and left.

What civil potentate, what opulent millionaire, what famous artist would do a thing like that? It would be to misinterpret the bishop of Rome's intention to see a populist intention in this action of his, so normal for all of us.

Didn't he do the same when he was archbishop of Buenos Aires, living in a small flat and not in the bishop's palace, and going out to buy his newspaper, buying what he was going to make to eat, traveling by bus or metro, and preferring to present himself as Father Bergoglio?

Frei Betto in Brazil has coined an expression that expresses a great truth: "The head thinks from where the feet tread." Indeed, if someone always walks in palaces and sumptuous cathedrals, he ends up thinking with the logic of palaces and cathedrals. That is why Francis celebrated mass one Sunday in the small church of Santa Ana, the Roman parish church of the pope in the Vatican. On another Sunday, which was celebrating the first communion for boys and girls, after mass he went up to them to hug and kiss them. While they sang the blessing of Saint Francis of Assisi over him, he remained the whole time with his head bowed, a sign of respect for that blessing and for the children.

In a remarkable gesture laden with theological meaning, he did not present himself as pope but as bishop of Rome. He asked for prayers for the bishop emeritus of Rome, Pope Benedict XVI. Thus he took up the church's oldest tradition again, which considers the bishop of Rome to be first among equals. Because Rome was the city where Peter and Paul are buried, it had special prominence. But this symbolic and spiritual power was exercised in charity and not in the form of legal power over the other churches, as was the dominant form in the second millennium.

It would not be surprising if one day, as John Paul II wanted, the pope should decide to abandon the Vatican and go off and live in a modest lodging, with plenty of outside space to receive visits from the faithful. The times are ripe for this type of revolution in papal customs. His example is challenging the other prelates of the church to live in voluntary simplicity and in shared restraint, close to the people they are meant to serve, encourage, and guide in the faith.

Francis, a Pope
Who Will Preside in Charity

THE GRAVE MORAL CRISIS BESETTING the whole institutional body of the church drove the conclave to elect someone with the authority and courage to carry out deep reforms in the Roman curia, and in the papacy itself, and to preside over the church more in charity and less in legal authority that weakens local churches. This is what the new pope, Francis, indicated when he pronounced his first words. If this happens, he will be the pope for the third millennium, and he will start a new dynasty of popes coming from the peripheries of Christendom: from Latin America, Africa, and Asia.

The figure of the pope is perhaps the greatest symbol of the sacred in the Western world. Modern societies have rid themselves of the sacred through secularization; they exhibit a deep nostalgia for the disappearing father figure, a father whose mission is to guide, create trust, give a sense of boundaries, show his sons and daughters safe and ethical ways. These ancestral desires are projected onto the figure of the pope, as an attentive observer could see in the faces of the faithful in Saint Peter's Square.

In that spirit Pope Francis broke the mold. He felt himself to be a man of the people, paying his bill in the hotel where he stayed, driving an ordinary car to the basilica of Santa Maria Maggiore, and keeping the iron cross he wears on his breast. He stands as the figure of the great Father, tender and strong, firm and kind.

For Christians the ministry of Peter has to be a focus for unity, and above all, it must strengthen the brothers and sisters in faith, according to the command of its Master. Rome, where Peter and Paul are buried, was from the beginning a focus for the confirmation of the gospel message and zeal for the other churches. This perspective is accepted today even by the non-Catholic churches. Everything rests on the way that office is exercised.

During a vacancy of imperial power, Pope Leo the Great (440–61) had to take on the government of Rome to confront Attila's Huns, who were advancing to threaten the city. He adopted the titles of pope and supreme pontiff, which belonged exclusively to the emperor, and incorporated the trappings of imperial, monarchical, and centralized power with its symbols, vestments, and palatial style.

The texts referring to Peter, in which Jesus meant service and love, were interpreted by Pope Leo the Great in the Roman style strictly as legal power. Everything came to a head with Gregory VII, who in 1075, with his *Dictatus Papae* (dictatorship of the pope) assumed both powers: the religious and the secular. There arose the "total institution," an obstacle to the freedom of Christians and currently an obstacle to ecumenism and dialogue with the modern globalized world.

That absolutist exercise of power was always questioned by theologians, especially by the reformers, but it was never softened. As John Paul II recognized in his document on ecumenism, that way of exercising the office of Peter is the greatest obstacle to church unity and to acceptance by those Christians who come from the democratic world. So it must be rethought. It is not enough to turn the faith into a spectacle with grand events to make up for what else is lacking.

The present monarchical form must be redefined in the light of Jesus' original intention, according to which all power must be service and free from all pomp. That is something done by pagans and the powerful of this world. "It will not be so among you" (Mt 20:26), Jesus insisted, but that is how it ended up.

Surely Pope Francis will introduce a pastoral, participatory style based on solidarity rather than authority in his exercise of sacred power. The Second Vatican Council established the tools to do so: *the synod of bishops*, which up until now has remained a consultative body, was meant to make decisions, and must become an executive body through which the pope governs the church; and *the collegiality of bishops*, that is, the continental and national conferences, the bishops as a body, which were intended to have more autonomy to enable the faith to become rooted in local cultures while remaining in communion with Rome.

It is not unthinkable that representatives of the people of God, from cardinals to women, should be invited to elect a pope for the whole of Christian world. It is urgent to reform the curia so that it becomes decentralized. Surely Pope Francis will do this. Why can't the Pontifical Council for Interreligious Dialogue have its office in Asia? the Dicastery [Department] for Christian Unity in Geneva, near the World Council of Churches? the Pontifical Council for Promoting New Evangelization in a city of Africa? the Pontifical Council for Justice and Peace in Latin America? Direct means of communication, such as Skype, video conferencing, blogs, Facebook, and so on make it possible to keep in touch online.

The Catholic Church could become a non-authoritarian purveyor of universal values, of human rights and of the rights of Mother Earth and nature against consumeristic culture and in support of shared moderation and solidarity.

The central question is not now the survival of the church but of humanity and civilization. These are the ecological and social threats that face us. How can the church help?

All this decentralization is possible without giving up any of the substance of the Christian faith. It is important that Pope Francis should be a John XXIII for a new time, a *good pope*, as he is showing himself to be. Only thus can he restore the church's lost credibility and be a beacon of spirituality and hope for all.

The risen Jesus Christ with his Spirit will not let Peter's boat capsize. It will withstand the threatening winds and waves. It will make a successful crossing toward a port of hope with renewed vigor.

Francis of Assisi Strips to Clothe the Nakedness of Pope Innocent III

HISTORY TELLS US THAT THE pope at the time of Saint Francis, Innocent III (1198–1216)—an intelligent man; a doctor of theology from the best school of the period, Paris; a legal expert, impressive orator, and crafty negotiator; elevated to the throne of Saint Peter at the age of thirty-seven—raised the papacy to a pinnacle of splendor it had neither before nor since in the whole history of the church.

He was a clever politician and, throughout Europe as far as Russia, he succeeded in making kings, emperors, and feudal lords (except a few) his vassals. Under his rule the two super powers were united: the empire and the pontificate.

It was not enough for him to be the successor of Peter, the fisherman. He declared himself to be Christ's representative. But he was not thinking of the poor Christ, who walked the dusty roads of Palestine. Nor was he considering the pilgrim prophet, announcing a radical utopia, the reign of unconditional love of neighbor and of God, of universal justice, limitless fellowship, and boundless love. Innocent's Christ is the Pantocrator, lord of the universe, head of the church and the cosmos, the universal king. This was the king whose representative and lieutenant he felt himself to be.

That vision fostered the creation of a monarchical church, which was rich and powerful but secularized, contrary to everything Jesus wanted from his apostles, who were sent out to preach carrying nothing, no purse, no money.

This expression of temporal power was bound to provoke a contrary reaction among simple and pious people. So pauper movements of men and women of the people arose, including rich laypeople who became poor. For their part, they preached the gospel in colloquial language: the gospel of poverty against the magnificence of royal courts, of radical simplicity against the sophistication of palaces, of worship of the Christ of Bethlehem and the cross against the exaltation of Christ the almighty King. These were the Albigenses, the Valdenses, the poor of Lyons, the followers of Saint Francis, of Saint Dominic, and of the Florentine Seven Servants of Mary, noblemen who became beggars.

Despite his splendor, Innocent III was touched by Francis and his eleven ragged companions, who visited him in his Roman palace, seeking permission to live in accordance with the gospel. Moved and remorseful, the pope granted them oral permission. It was the year 1209. Francis never forgot that generous gesture.

But history has its ups and downs. When the moment comes, what is true and imperative is revealed and will brook no denial. This happened on July 16, 1216, in Perugia, where Pope Innocent III had one of his palaces.

The pope died suddenly after eighteen years of his triumphant papacy. Then mournful sounds of Gregorian chant were heard in the pontifical cathedral. They intoned the solemn *planctum super Innocentium* (lament for Innocent). No one can stop death, sovereign lady above all vanities, pomp, glory, and triumph. The pope's coffin lay in front of the high altar, covered in rich gold and silver ornaments and jewels, signs of his double sacred and civil power. Cardinals, emperors, princes, abbots, and endless queues of the faithful filed past to contemplate the pope's mortal remains. So we are told by Bishop Jacques de Vitry, who had come from Namur and who afterward became cardinal of Frascati.

It is midnight. All have mournfully retired. Only the flickering candlelight projects phantoms on the walls. Now the dead pope, who all his life was surrounded by nobles, is wrapped only in darkness. His own servants, who know all about the jewels set in silver and gold and placed in the papal coffin, enter the cathedral secretly, and within a few minutes they have stripped his corpse of all his precious vestments, the gold, the silver, and the papal insignia.

His naked body lay there almost in a state of decomposition. There lay what Innocent had described in a famous text on the misery of the human condition—starkly on view in the condition of the pope himself.

A poor, dirty, wretched little man was hiding in a dark corner of the cathedral to keep vigil, pray, and spend the night beside the pope, who in 1209 had approved his dream of a life lived in accordance with the gospel in poverty and simplicity. He took off his torn and dirty tunic, his penitential tunic, and used it to cover the nakedness of the violated corpse. It was Francis of Assisi, who stripped bare to cover his friend the pope's nakedness.

Wealth's sad fate! Poverty's grand gesture! The former did not save him from being plundered. The latter saved him from shame. And Cardinal Jacques de Vitry concludes: "I entered the church and I realized with total faith how short and deceitful is the glory of this world."

Pope Francis does not run the same risk as Innocent III. As bishop and cardinal he has always adopted poverty as a personal option and rejected all splendor as a way of life. There is nothing in Francis that can inspire the covetousness of those who live with him. Indeed, he challenges all Christians to become less consumeristic, to live more simply, and to treat one another as brothers and sisters, which we really are because we are all sons and daughters of God, who is Father and Mother of infinite goodness. In this way the pope is ahead of us. It is up to us to follow his example.

The Ecology of Francis of Assisi and Francis of Rome

IT IS VERY SIGNIFICANT THAT a pope should take the name Francis. As well as referring to another way of being church, closer to the Bethlehem cave than the Jerusalem palaces, Francis of Assisi raises a subject that is extremely urgent for us today: the question of caring for the life of the earth and guaranteeing the future of our civilization. For this, external ecology is not enough. We have to join it with internal ecology. And that is what Francis of Assisi did in a paradigmatic way.

External ecology is the fine-tuning we develop in accord with the rhythms of nature and the cosmic process that occurs in the dialectic of order–disorder–interaction– new order. This ecology guarantees the continuation of the evolutionary process, which includes the universe, the earth, and biodiversity. This ecology is also called environmental because it takes care of our natural environment (which is always the whole environment) of water, soil, forests, flora, and fauna in order to safeguard its integrity.

But on the human level, external ecology can only be maintained if we give something for our part, something derived from internal ecology. For the universe and its creatures are inside us in the form of symbols that speak to us, archetypes that guide us, and powerful images that dwell in our minds, all matter with which we must continually converse and that we must integrate. If there is violence in external ecology (in families and society), this is a sign that there is turbulence in our internal ecology (in our psychology and state of mind) and vice versa. We do not know how to harmonize the ecologies: the environment, the social, the mental, and the integral.

In "Canticle of the Creatures," Saint Francis reveals the convergence of the external and the internal ecologies. His extraordinary spiritual achievement was to reconcile the universe with God, heaven with earth, life with death.

In order to understand this experience of totality, we have to go beyond the literal sense of the text and reach down to the symbolic level, where the elements of the song are impregnated with feeling and meaning.

The existential context is significant: Francis was very ill, swollen with malaria, almost blind, and being looked after by Saint Clare in a hut beside the small church of San Damiano where she was living with her sisters. Suddenly, in the middle of the night, he had a sort of exaltation of spirit, as if he were already in the kingdom of heaven. Radiant with joy, he got up and composed a canticle to all creatures, inviting his brothers and sisters to sing with him.

The canticle celebrates the great marriage between Lord Brother Sun and Lady Sister Earth. From this marriage all creatures are born, ordered in pairs, masculine and feminine, which, according to C. G. Jung, constitute the most universal archetype of psychic wholeness: sun-moon, wind-water, fire-earth.

The canticle contains two more stanzas added by Francis. In them, the song is not about the material cosmos but about the human world, which also seeks reconciliation—Bishop Guido of Assisi meeting the mayor. Finally, there is reconciliation with Sister Death, the most difficult complex to integrate for the human psyche. Life embraces death as a sister and bearer of eternity.

Internal ecology integrated with external ecology finds a privileged interpreter in Francis. He is like a very fine string of the universe on which the most subtle musical note is played and heard.

Our culture has chosen the way of Saint Francis's father, Pedro Bernardone, a rich cloth merchant, seeker of wealth and splendor. Arnold Toynbee, the great English historian, confesses, "Francis, the greatest man ever to live in the West must be imitated by all of us, because his attitude is the only one that can save the earth, not that of his father, the merchant Bernardone" (ABC, Madrid, December 19, 1972, 10).

What do we want? That Francis of Rome should take his inspiration from Francis of Assisi and be transformed through his humility, poverty, and cheerfulness into a lover of Mother Earth and a defender of all kinds of life, especially lives that are most threatened—the lives of the poor and those who suffer most—and that he should raise this awareness in humanity. In him are present all the charisms that can make him become a shining humanitarian and ecological lighthouse for the whole world, beyond all current religions and ideologies.

Pope Francis,
Promoter of Ecological Awareness

WE ARE BECOMING MORE AND more aware that we are entering a dangerous period in the life of the earth. Dark clouds cover our guiding stars and warn us of possible ecological-social tsunamis, especially at the moment when we pass the red line of four hundred parts per million of carbon dioxide in the atmosphere of some regions in the North.

Unfortunately, we lack leaders with authority, convincing words, and deeds to wake people up, especially the governing elites, to the common destiny of the earth and humanity and the collective and diverse responsibility to guarantee it for all.

In this context the figure of Francis, bishop of Rome, can play a very relevant part. He explicitly relates to the figure of Saint Francis of Assisi. First, he does so through his clear option for the poor—a stance against poverty and for social justice. That option first arose within the Latin American liberation church and theology of the people at the assemblies of the bishops of Latin American at Medellín, Colombia (1968), and Puebla, Mexico (1978). According to John Paul II, it has become the patrimony of the universal church.

This option, as liberation theologians have understood very well, includes the planet, which is in such distress now that our environmental impact is so great that the earth needs a year and a half to replace what we take out for our consumption in one year.

This fact brings us to the ecological question, that is, how should we relate to nature and to Mother Earth? Here, Francis of Assisi can inspire Francis of Rome. There are elements in the practical life of Francis of Assisi that are sources of inspiration. Let us look at some of them.

All the biographers of his time (Celano, Saint Bonaventure, the Legend of Perugia, and others) testify to the most tender affection he had for creatures; he gave them the kind name of brothers and sisters. He read their secrets as if he already enjoyed the freedom and glory of the children of God. He freed birds from their cages, took care of wounded animals, and even begged gardeners to leave a corner uncultivated, so that weeds could grow, since "they too proclaim the most beautiful Father of all creatures."

Here we see another way of being in the world, different from our modern one, in which human beings set themselves *above* things to possess and dominate them. Francis's way is to stand *beside* them, to live together as brothers and sisters at home. He sensed mystically what we know today from scientific data: we all carry the same basic genetic code. So we are blood relations, parents, cousins, brothers, and sisters of one another. Hence the importance of respecting and loving one another and never using violence against our fellow human beings or other creatures, who are our brothers and sisters.

Saint Francis is closer to indigenous peoples, like the Yanomami or the Andeans, who feel themselves to be part of nature, than to the sons and daughters of technical-scientific modernity, who regard nature as wild and at our disposal to be tamed and exploited.

The whole of modernity has been constructed almost exclusively on intellectual intelligence, which, of course, has brought us countless conveniences. But it has not made us more integrated or happier, because it has relegated the heart's intelligence, emotional intelligence, to a subordinate level and denied citizenship to spiritual intelligence. Today it is urgent to articulate these three expressions of intelligence if we want to sort out the values and feelings that depend on them: reverence, respect, and peaceful coexistence with nature and the earth.

This effort will put us in tune with the logic of nature itself, which marries and inter-retro-connects everybody with everything. It will mean living in symbiosis with other living things and sustaining the subtle web of life.

Francis lived out this synthesis between internal and external ecology to the point where Saint Bonaventure called him *homo alterius saeculi*—a man of another age—or, as we would say today, another paradigm.

This attitude will be fundamental for the future of our civilization, of nature, and of life on earth. Francis of Rome must become the bearer of this sacred legacy, bequeathed by Francis of Assisi to all humanity. The bishop of Rome can help different societies to move from our current type of world, which can destroy us, to a different one, already anticipated by Saint Francis, a world of cosmic fellowship, unconditional tenderness, and love, in a word, a society that sustains all life.

Without these values it will be difficult for us to move from the threat of tragedy to a cathartic crisis. It will be an alliance of peace and synergy between human beings and nature, between techno-science and Mother Earth, which will give rise to a new way of inhabiting the only common household we have, the earth. It will be a triumph of the paradigm of care over the paradigm of domination, the victory of a feeling heart over a cold and conquering mind. We need the three forms of intelligence—intellectual, emotional, and spiritual—in order to live like human beings. Together, we can develop the sensitivity and love that are vital to all that exists and lives. Then everything will be in ecological harmony, that is, linked and interwoven to form the great community of creatures and of life.

We hope that Pope Francis, inspired by Saint Francis of Assisi, will be able to become the great promoter of ecological awareness and of responsible solidarity for the common destiny of earth and humanity, a destiny that must be happy and radically human.

Will Pope Francis Inaugurate the Church of the Third Millennium?

THE FIRST MILLENNIUM OF CHRISTIANITY was marked by the paradigm of community. The local churches had relative autonomy, with their own rituals: the Orthodox, the Coptic, the Ambrosian in Milan, the Mozarabic in Spain, and others. They venerated their own martyrs and confessors and had their own theologies, as can be seen in the flourishing Christianity of North Africa with Saint Augustine, Saint Cyprian, and lay theologian and eminent lawyer Tertullian. They gave each other mutual recognition, and the bishop of Rome presided over them in charity, assuming the title of pope. Nevertheless, very early on, signs could be seen of a legalistic vision inherited from Roman culture with its elaborate Roman law.

The second millennium was characterized by the paradigm of the church as a perfect, hierarchical society: an absolute monarchy centered on the person of the pope as the supreme head, endowed with limitless powers, and even infallible when he pronounces as such on matters of faith or morals. The Papal States were established, with an army, a financial system, and a legal system that included the death penalty, carried out on various occasions.

A body of institutional experts was created, the Roman curia, responsible for the administration of the church worldwide. This centralization caused the Romanization of the whole of Christianity. The evangelization of Latin America, Asia, and Africa took place within a process of colonial conquest of the world, which subjugated indigenous populations and looted their natural riches.

The evangelization practiced was a transfer of the Roman model, which practically annihilated any embodiment in local cultures. The separation between clergy and laity became official. The latter were deprived of all decision-making power, whereas during the first millennium they had taken part in the election of bishops and of the pope himself. Legally and in practice they were relegated to inferiority.

The palatial customs of priests, bishops, cardinals, and popes became entrenched. The power titles of the Roman emperors, beginning with the titles of pope and supreme pontiff, passed to the bishop of Rome, who from then on presented himself as pope and above all the other local and national churches.

Cardinals became princes of the church and dressed like the Renaissance high nobility, a custom that has continued up to our time, scandalizing Christians who see Jesus as a poor man of the people, persecuted, tortured, and executed on the cross.

Everything indicates that this church model has come to an end with the resignation of Benedict XVI, the last pope to reign in this monarchical style, and in a tragic context of scandals within the church itself, which have affected the core credibility and trustworthiness of the Christian message.

The election of Pope Francis, who comes from the periphery of Christianity in the South, home to 60 percent of Catholics, seems to inaugurate the ecclesial paradigm for the third millennium: the church as a huge network of Christian communities rooted in different cultures, some more ancient than Western culture, such as China, India, Japan, the tribal cultures of Africa, and the communitarian cultures of Latin America.

The church is embodied in the modern culture of technically advanced countries and elsewhere in regions that have already adopted modernity. It is also embodied in popular culture, particularly on the peripheries where the ecclesial base communities are mainly, but not exclusively, to be found, as well as the pastoral-social networks and the various popular movements in which many Christians take part. All these incarnations face a common challenge: the urbanization of humanity with more than 60 percent of the population (83 percent in Brazil) live in great conurbations of millions of inhabitants.

In this context it is practically impossible to speak of territorial parishes, like those in country districts. Parishes will now be neighborhood communities, or communities based on a building or nearby streets. The protagonists of this Christianity will be the laity, men and women, encouraged by priests, who have more to do with fostering faith than with administration. The churches will have new configurations and new faces.

The reform will not be confined to the Roman curia, which is in a disastrous state, but will extend to the whole church institution and to the papacy itself. Perhaps reformation will come by the calling of a new council with representatives of the whole of Christianity, laity, men, and women of all Christian churches, distinguished by their knowledge, and representatives from other religions and spiritual paths. A council with this scope and such wide representation will give the pope the necessary clout to face resistance and will set out the guidelines for the Catholic Church and perhaps for the other Christian churches for the third millennium.

May the Holy Spirit blow strongly on these initiatives. Pentecost, which descended like a rushing wind upon the apostles, has not yet come to an end. It was just the beginning. Pope Francis will need divine light and inspiration from the Spirit of life, Father of the poor, and Light of hearts to preside over this crossing, which is laden with risks but even more with promise and hope.

The Temptations of Francis of Assisi and Francis of Rome

WE CERTAINLY SHOULD NOT IMAGINE that the saints were free from the influences of the common human condition, which knows moments of exaltation and frustration, dangerous temptations, and courageous victories. It was no different for Saint Francis, presented as "the ever joyful brother," always courteous, who lived in mystic fusion with all creatures, who were brothers and sisters to him. However, at the same time, he was someone beset by great passions and fierce rages when he saw his ideals betrayed by his own brothers. His best biographer, Thomas of Celano, relates with cruel realism that Francis suffered temptations to violent injury, which he was able to sublimate symbolically.

However, there is a detail the pious historiography of the Franciscans almost covers up, but that historical criticism has investigated very thoroughly under the name of the "great temptation." The last five years of Francis's life (he died in 1226) were marked by deep, almost desperate anxieties, as well as by terrible pains that mortified him, such as malaria, and perhaps leprosy and blindness. The problem was objective: his ideal of life was to live in extreme poverty, radical simplicity, and stripped of any power, relying solely on the gospel, read without any of the interpretations that usually soften its revolutionary meaning.

Within a few years his lifestyle attracted thousands of followers, more than five thousand. How could they be housed? How could they be fed? Many were priests and theologians, like Saint Anthony of Bologna. Francis's movement had neither structure nor legal status. It was a dream taken seriously. Francis regarded even himself as *novellus pazzus*—a new madman—who sought God in a very rich church, ruled by Innocent III, the most powerful pope in history.

From the summer of 1220 he wrote various versions of the rule, which were all rejected by the brotherhood as a whole. They were too utopian. In particular, Friar Elias, a pragmatic and not very spiritual man appointed coordinator of the movement, grumbled irritably to Francis: "Make a rule just for yourself; don't impose such a hard one on us."

Frustrated and feeling useless, he decided to give up the leadership of the movement. Distressed and not knowing what to do, he took refuge in a forest for two years. He was visited only by his intimate friend Friar Leo. With many tears and prayers he waited for divine illumination, which was a long time coming.

During this interval a rule was drawn up, strongly influenced by the Roman curia and the pope, which transformed the movement into a religious order, the Order of Friars Minor, with clearly defined structure and purposes. Francis humbly and painfully accepted this, but he made it clear he would no longer discuss it but would speak by example, showing how he still kept within him his original dream of poverty, simplicity, humility, and faithful following of Christ, who was poor and crucified.

Law triumphed over life, and power blocked charism. This is what usually happens in history to great charismatic movements. They end up being absorbed by the institution. This quite often makes way for the mediocre.

The spirit of Francis survives and can still inspire us today. He died amid great personal frustration but without losing his cheerfulness. He died singing Provençal love songs in French and psalms in Latin.

Doubtless, Francis of Rome will be facing his "great temptation," no less than did Francis of Assisi. He will have to reform the Roman curia, an institution that has lasted nearly a thousand years, in which sacred power *(sacra potestas)* is crystallized in administrative form. After all, it is about administering an institution with a population as large as China's: 1.2 billion Catholics. But we should immediately note that where there is power it is difficult for love and compassion to flourish. We get the reign of doctrine, order, and law, which by their nature include or exclude, approve or condemn.

Where there is power, especially in an absolute monarchy like the Vatican State, anti-power always arises, with intrigues, ambition, and struggles for more power. In his *Leviathan* (1651) Thomas Hobbes saw clearly: "Power cannot be guaranteed except by seeking power and more power."

Francis of Rome, the present local bishop and pope, will have to interfere in this power, imbued with a thousand cunning plans and sometimes acts of corruption. We know from previous popes and the history of the papacy that those who tried to reform the Roman curia met with fierce resistance and great frustration. There were even suspicions that some popes were physically eliminated by Mafioso types who infiltrated into the ecclesiastical administration.

Francis of Rome has something of the spirit of Saint Francis of Assisi; he is for poverty, simplicity, and total stripping away of power. And fortunately for us, he is a Jesuit with a different education, endowed with the famous discernment of spirits belonging to his order. At every crucial moment the Jesuit asks himself: What does God want of me? What decision must I take? In his decisions, we may hope, Pope Francis will try to unite the tenderness that he explicitly shows with unusual vigor with the desire to fulfill the mission with which he has been entrusted to restore the church that is morally in ruins.

Francis of Assisi had a few advisers, who were dreamers like himself and did not know how to give him practical help. Francis of Rome is surrounded by advisers chosen from every continent. They are mostly quite old, that is, experienced in the exercise of sacred power. Now this power must acquire a different face, one more of service than command, stripped down rather than adorned with palatial symbols, having the smell of sheep rather than the scent of altar flowers.

The bearer of sacred power must be a pastor rather than an ecclesiastical authority; he must preside more in charity and less with the coldness of canon law; he must be a brother among brothers and sisters, even though with different responsibilities.

Inspired by his namesake from Assisi, will Francis of Rome withstand his great temptation? I think he will be able to keep a firm hand and will not lack courage to follow what his discernment of spirit tells him in order to restore the church's credibility and renew enthusiasm for the figure of Jesus.

Being Radically Poor to Become Altogether a Brother

ONE OF THE FIRST STATEMENTS by Pope Francis was that he would like "a poor church for the poor." That desire accords with the spirit of Saint Francis, the Poverello, the Little Poor Man of Assisi. He did not try to run a church for the poor, because that would have been impossible in the Christendom regime, where the whole church was organized around sacred and civil power. But he created a community of poor people around himself, with the poor and like the poor.

In terms of his class background, Francis of Assisi belonged to the influential local bourgeoisie. His father was a rich cloth merchant, who traveled with Francis to trade fairs in the South of France and Holland. Through these journeys Francis learned the French language spoken in Languedoc in southern France, especially the songs and performances of the strolling players. Francis of Rome comes from a lower-class background and has always said he supported Peronism with its Justicialist (Perón's movement) tendency, seeking justice and fairness for all.

When he was young, Francis of Assisi was the leader of a group of rich, Bohemian friends—golden youth— who lived from party to party, drinking, singing, and laughing rowdily into the early mornings. When he grew up he went through an existential crisis from which he emerged into inexplicable compassion and love for the poor, especially lepers, who were kept incommunicado outside the city.

He left his family and business and took up radical gospel poverty. He went off to live with lepers. The poor crucified Jesus and the poor people around him were the strongest motives for his change of life. He spent two years in prayer and doing penance until he heard within him the call of the crucified Christ: "Francis, go and restore my house, because it is in ruins."

He did not initially understand that this was not about something material but a spiritual mission. He set off along the roads, preaching the gospel in colloquial language from village to village. He did it with such cheerfulness, grace, and conviction that he stirred some of his former companions. In 1209 he received approval from Pope Innocent III for his gospel "madness." The Franciscan movement had begun; in less than twenty years it had gathered more than five thousand followers.

The movement was structured around four central points: passionate love for the crucified Christ, tender and brotherly love for the poor (Lady Poverty), genuine simplicity, and great humility.

Leaving aside the other points, we want to concentrate here on how Francis saw and lived with the poor, because that is an important subject for us today. In fact, he didn't do anything *for* the poor (a leper house or charitable work), but he did a lot *with* the poor, since he included them in his preaching of the gospel, and wherever he could be, he was with them. But what he did most was live *like* the poor. He adopted their way of life and customs, kissed them, cleaned their wounds, and ate with them. He became poor among the poor. And if he met anyone poorer than himself, he gave that person some of his clothes, so that he would be the poorest of all.

For Francis, poverty did not mean not having, but rather giving more and more, until he gave everything. It was an ascetic path but a way of seeking incomparable excellence: identification with Christ who was poor and with the poor themselves in a relationship of brotherhood.

Francis had realized that property comes between people, preventing a meeting heart to heart and face to face. Those *interests*, a word that comes from the Latin *inter esse*, "to be among," separate us from others and create obstacles to brotherhood. He became radically poor in order to become brother. That was Francis's project of poverty.

Such radical poverty was very hard. No one can live on mysticism alone. Bodily life in the world has requirements that cannot be avoided. How can the real dehumanization that is present in this type of poverty be humanized? Sources of the period testify that the friars seemed like *silvestres homines* (wild men). They ate very little, went about barefoot, and dressed in the most miserable clothes. But to the surprise of all, they never lost their cheerfulness and good humor.

In this context of extreme poverty Francis values fellowship and caring. The poor challenge others to take care of them and to seek to provide, through giving or through work, the minimum necessary for their shelter and security. So *having* becomes trying to give security and humanity. Francis wants every friar to be like a mother to others, because mothers take special care of the sick.

Only a caring relationship humanizes existence, as Martin Heidegger showed clearly in *Being and Time* (1927). For anyone living without protection, fellowship meant everything. Francis's biographer, Thomas of Celano, describes the cheerfulness and joy there was amid such bleak poverty, saying: "They longed to meet each other; they were happy when they could be together, distance was painful, parting was bitter, separation was sad." Having nothing enabled them to enjoy the beauty of everything, because they did not want to possess, only to relish.

This spiritual adventure could teach us many lessons, but let us focus on one: for Francis of Assisi, human relationships must always be built upon those who are nothing and have nothing according to the view of the powerful. These poor people must be embraced as sisters and brothers. Only fellow feeling surging up from below and then enfolding everyone is truly human, universal, and sustainable.

The church, as we have it today, will never be *like* the poor, but it can be *for* and *with* the poor. The motherly behavior Francis of Assisi wanted in his friars is what Pope Francis wants to see in pastors. They are not to be administrators but pastors who care for, feed, and treat the faithful with affection.

This means having less in order to be more, consuming with solidarity so that all can consume the necessary, and with dignity, adopting shared restraint against a culture of accumulation and waste.

The favorite subject of the current pope is poverty. With poverty come attitudes of meeting, living together, listening, dialogue, and compassion for the poor. He has said clearly that poverty cannot be overcome with philanthropy but only with social justice. In his speech in the community of Varginha, he showed how he personally lived with poverty: he entered a modest house, had coffee with the family, hugged the children and the old people, and conveyed clearly that he felt as if he were in his own home.

He spoke to the cardinals and bishops present of the need to care and for a *revolution of tenderness.* This is a molecular revolution taking place. It can envelop the whole church and more and more people in society, in order to make possible a huge and necessary change of civilization: the closeness of each to all, respect, shared restraint, and care for life that is threatened.

Liberation Theology
and Theology of the People

MANY HAVE WONDERED WHETHER, SINCE the present Pope Francis comes from Latin America, he is a supporter of liberation theology. The question is irrelevant. The important thing is not to be for liberation theology but for the liberation of the oppressed, the poor, and the victims of injustice, and that he is without question.

In fact, this was always the purpose of liberation theology. Real liberation from hunger, poverty, moral degradation, and distance from God comes first. That reality belongs to the benefits of the kingdom of God and is what Jesus intended. Reflection on these real things comes second: to what extent can the kingdom of God be brought about in anticipation and in what way can Christianity, with its spiritual potential inherited from Jesus, collaborate with other humanitarian groups in this necessary liberation?

Later reflection, called theology, may or may not exist. The decisive thing is that the fact of real liberation should occur. There will always be attentive spirits who hear the cry of the oppressed and of the devastated earth and ask themselves: from what we have learned from Jesus, the apostles, and Christian doctrine over so many centuries, how can we contribute to the process of liberation? That was what a whole generation of Christians did, from cardinals to laymen and laywomen from the 1960s on. They continue to do so today, because the poor continue to increase, and their cry has become a roar.

Pope Francis has lived liberation theology among us. That is a way of doing theology more than that found at any school. It starts from the cry of the oppressed and thinks and acts for liberation. Pope Francis has taken this option for the poor; he has lived and continues to live in solidarity with them and has said very clearly that he would like "a poor church for the poor." In this sense Pope Francis is fulfilling the primordial insight of liberation theology and promoting its registered trademark: the preferential option for the poor and in favor of life and justice.

For him, this option is not just rhetoric but a life choice and a spirituality. For the sake of the poor he has fallen out with the public authorities in Argentina in order to commit himself politically to the overcoming of social problems. Analytically these problems are called inequalities, ethically they represent injustices, and theologically they constitute social sin. This directly calls out to God, who showed in the Bible that God is always on the side of those who have the least life and are victims of injustice.

In 1990, 4 percent of people in Argentina were poor. Today, given the voracity of national and international capital, nearly 20 percent are poor. These are not just numbers. For a sensitive and spiritual person like Pope Francis, these facts represent a whole load of suffering, tears of hungry children, and desperation of unemployed parents. It reminds me of something Dostoyevsky said: "All the progress in the world is not worth the crying of a hungry child."

As Pope Francis has insisted, this poverty cannot be overcome by philanthropy but by public policies that restore dignity to the oppressed and make them autonomous and participating citizens.

It doesn't matter that Pope Francis does not use the expression "liberation theology." The important thing is that he speaks and acts in a liberating way. In Argentina a tendency developed, not as an alternative to liberation theology but as a typical expression of the local culture: a theology of the people or *theology of popular culture*. The people under Juan Domingo Perón developed a high level of political consciousness and created a rich and popular culture participating in the destiny of the nation. According to Jesuit Father Juan Carlos Scannone, the main exponent of this kind of theology, Jorge Mario Bergoglio (later to become Pope Francis) was a student of his in the Colegio Maximo de San Miguel in the suburbs of Buenos Aires. Father Bergoglio always supported this theology of the people. So, without having to use the more common expression "liberation theology," he never departed from his basic insight and fundamental aim: to make the faith an instrument for the liberation of the oppressed. Instead of doing a class analysis showing the origins of impoverishment and social oppression, theology of the people prefers to analyze popular culture in its dynamism and its contradictions, stressing the elements of participation and liberation that are present in it.

The two tendencies complement each other in the service of a very important cause: the difficult service, demanding sacrifice, and sometimes even martyrdom of supporting the poor in their struggles and strengthening their desire for liberation.

It is also right that a pope should not affiliate himself with a single type of theology, like liberation theology, theology of the people, or any other. His two predecessors held to a certain type of theology that presented itself as an expression of the official magisterium. In its name a good number of theologians, about five hundred—both men and women—were condemned over the period of more than twenty years that Cardinal Joseph Ratzinger presided over the Congregation for the Doctrine of the Faith. The different forms of condemnation or censure created an atmosphere of distrust and fear within the church, which was harmful both to theological reflection and to pastoral practice.

Historians know that the category *magisterium*, attributed to the popes and always invoked by them, is a recent creation. Pope Gregory XVI (1831–46) and Pope Pius X (1903–14) began its use, and it became common with Pius XII (1939–58). Before that the magisterium was made up of doctors and professors of theology, not bishops and the pope, who are teachers of the faith. Theologians are teachers of the *understanding* of the faith. So it was not the job of bishops and popes to do theology, but rather to witness to it officially and jealously guarantee the Christian faith. It is the job of theologians to deepen this witness with the intellectual tools offered by their culture.

When popes start doing theology, as happened recently, we do not know whether they are speaking as popes or as theologians. There is great confusion in the church, and freedom of research and dialogue with different disciplines are lost.

Thanks be to God, Pope Francis presents himself openly as a pastor and not as a doctor and theologian, either of liberation or of the people. This makes him freer to speak from the standpoint of the gospel, with his emotional and spiritual intelligence, with an open and feeling heart, in tune with the globalized world of today.

May Pope Francis put theology in a minor key so that liberation may ring out in a major key, as a comfort for the oppressed and as a call to the consciences of the powerful. What we need is less theology and more liberation.

A Committed and Fearless Faith
in Pope Francis

THE ENCYCLICAL *LUMEN FIDEI*, ADOPTED jointly by the pope emeritus and Pope Francis, was not reflected in the speeches made in Brazil. The encyclical has neither the tone nor the language of the present pope. In Brazil he bore witness to the Christian faith without the theological sophistication to be found in *Lumen Fidei.* He used direct language both with the young and with intellectuals.

So let us reflect on the faith from a very human perspective, which even someone who does not profess any faith should understand. Many people have said publicly that the faith as presented by Pope Francis is respectable and worthy of consideration for modern and enlightened reasons.

Nevertheless, we have to recognize that at present the question of faith does not loom large in social and philosophical thought. On the contrary, most thinkers who are children of modernity are suspicious of it and consider it to be an archaic and mythical way of thinking or the uninformed and unscientific cosmovision of the superstitious.

However we interpret the faith, the fact is that it is present and mobilizes millions of young people who came from all over the world to Brazil for the World Youth Day, as well as the thousands of others who came to see the new Pope Francis. I suspect no other ideology, cause, or nonreligious leader is capable of attracting such large multitudes in the streets. Can we responsibly say that this is an alienated and archaic faith? This leads us to reflect on the relevance of faith in people's lives.

In *A Rumor of Angels: Modern Society and the Rediscovery of the Supernatural* (1969) the widely known sociologist Peter Berger showed the fallacy of secularization that claimed to have banished religion and the sacred from the social sphere. Both have acquired new forms but are present because they are rooted deep in the fundamental needs of human life.

Imagining that human beings might one day totally abandon faith is as unlikely as expecting that in order not to consume chemical or genetically modified foodstuffs we stop eating forever. I want to approach faith in its most genuine sense, putting aside doctrines, dogmas, and religions, because this is where it appears at its most human.

There is a pre-reflexive given that underlies the existence of faith: trust in the fundamental goodness of life. However absurd it may be, human beings believe it is worth living rather than dying. I will give a simple example: a child wakes up with a start in the middle of the night. He cries out for his mother because he is scared of nightmare and darkness. His mother sits him on her lap, cuddles him, and says, "Don't be afraid, darling, everything is all right, everything is in order." The sobbing child gradually recovers and in a short while falls asleep. Is his mother deceiving her child? For really, everything is not all right. Nevertheless, we feel the mother is not lying to her child. Despite the contradictions, there is trust in a basic order permeating reality, so that it is not taken over by the absurd.

Believing is saying yes and amen to reality. Philosopher Ludwig Wittgenstein could say in his *Tractatus logico-philosophicus*: "Believing is affirming that life has meaning." That is the biblical sense of faith—*he 'emin ou aman*—which means "being sure and trusting." Hence comes the word *amen*, which means "so it is." Having faith is being sure of the meaning of life.

Such faith is a basic anthropological fact. We don't think about it because we live inside it; it is worth living and sacrificing ourselves to make a meaning that is worthwhile.

Saying that this meaning of life is *God* is the way religions put it. This meaning permeates people, society, and universe, despite our endless questions. Pope Francis wrote in the encyclical *Lumen Fidei:* "Faith is not a light which scatters all our darkness, but a lamp which guides our steps in the night and suffices for the journey" (no. 57).

Saying that this meaning, which is God, has come close to us and taken on our warm, mortal flesh in Jesus of Nazareth is what the Christian faith says. In the name of that faith in Jesus, who died and rose again, thousands of young people, and more than two million people in all, gathered in Copacabana.

A strong feature of Pope Francis's charisma is his limpid faith, which makes him appear so free and fearless (the opposite of faith is not atheism but fear). He tries to come close to people, especially the poor. Francis inspires what is proper to faith: the feeling of being in the palm of God's hand. He is the archetype of the good father who inspires trust.

He proclaimed an important message and gave a true lesson to many movements in Brazil: faith must keep its eyes open to the wounds of the poor, stay close to them, and be active in eradicating the causes of poverty.

Pope Francis stressed an evangelization that gets close to the people and the poor in simplicity and poverty, and he repeated, "Don't be afraid." Commitment to social justice creates conflicts and victims; it arouses fear that only faith can overcome.

Let's go back to the subject of human faith. Many people call themselves atheists and agnostics, but they still have faith; that is, they say yes to life, and they work for life to become just and in solidarity. Perhaps they profess this faith without explicit reference to God or Jesus Christ, but that is not the most important thing. What underlies faith in God and Jesus Christ is a reality that does not need to be spoken of.

This basic faith imposes limits on vulgar postmodernism that is not interested in a better humanity and is not committed to solidarity or concerned with the tragic fate of so many people who are suffering. When they see the fervent faith of so many young people, moved even to tears, others perhaps will feel nostalgia for their childhood faith. Then impulses may arise that encourage them to live by fundamental human faith. It is even possible that one day they may open up to faith in God and Jesus Christ. Faith is a gift, but it is the gift of a victory, with a greater meaning that gives human beings an opening into a happier life.

The Pope of Freedom of Spirit
and the Heart's Reason

One of the greatest gains for human beings in the process of individuation is freedom of spirit, which is the capacity to be doubly free: *free* of the conditionings, rules, and regulations invented by society and the institutions that instill uniform behavior and mold personality along these lines; and fundamentally *free* to be authentic, think our own thoughts, and act in accordance with our own conscience, which matures throughout life, in resistance and in tension with those conditionings.

This is a titanic battle. All of us are born determined by certain things independent of our own will, since family, school, circle of friends, religion, and culture form our habits. All these function as super-egos that can limit us and in some cases damage us. Certainly limits have an important regulatory function. The river reaches the sea because it has banks and borders. But these can also hold back the waters that should flow, and then they overflow the banks and become stagnant ponds.

The surprising attitudes and behavior of the present bishop of Rome, as he likes to present himself rather than as Pope Francis, show this vital freedom of spirit.

Normally the cardinal elected pope immediately takes on the classical sacral and hieratic style of the popes in vestments, gestures, language, and in the symbols of supreme sacred power. With great freedom of spirit Francis does the opposite; he adapts the figure of the pope to his personal style, his own habits, and his own convictions.

84

Everyone knows of the changes he has made without ceremony. He has renounced all the symbols of power, especially the golden cross and jewels, as well as the silk cape, the *mozzetta,* once the symbol of Roman emperors. He dresses quietly, in white, with his usual black shoes and trousers. He has given up all the perks belonging to the supreme office of the church, beginning with the papal apartment. He has exchanged that for a church guesthouse, where he eats together with the other residents. He thinks more about the poor Peter, a simple fisherman, and about Jesus, who was a simple Mediterranean peasant. Francis feels he is the successor of Peter and representative of Jesus. He does not want to be called Your Holiness, because he feels he is a brother among brothers. Neither does he want to rule the church with the rigor of canon law but rather with warm-hearted kindness.

On his trip to Brazil he unostentatiously showed his freedom of spirit by choosing for his transport an ordinary vehicle, a covered jeep, in which to move about among the people, hug children, drink a little maté. He even exchanged his white papal cap for a scruffy cap offered him by one of the faithful. After the speech in the official welcoming ceremony by the government, which follows a strict protocol, he went up to President Dilmma Rousseff and, to the dismay of the master of ceremonies, gave her a kiss. And we could give many more examples.

This freedom of spirit gives him an undeniable glow of tenderness and vigor, which were personal characteristics of Saint Francis. He is a man of great integrity. These strong, serene attitudes reveal a person of great sensibility who has achieved a significant synthesis between his deep "I" and his conscious "I." That is precisely what we hope for in a religious guide.

This freedom of spirit is empowered by his splendid restoration of the *heart's reason.* Most Christians are tired of doctrines and skeptical about campaigns against real or imaginary enemies of the faith. We are fed up to the teeth with intellectual, functional, analytic, and pragmatic reason. And now someone appears who always speaks from the heart, as he did in the *favela* of Varginha or on the Italian island of Lampedusa. The heart is the dwelling place of deep feeling toward others and toward God. When they lack heart, doctrines are cold and do not arouse any passion. In the face of the refugees from Africa on Lampedusa in July 2013 he said, "We are a society which has forgotten the experience of weeping, of 'suffering with'; the globalization of indifference has taken from us the ability to weep." And he wisely stated in Varginha on July 25, 2013: "The greatness of a society can be measured by the way in which it treats those most in need, those who have nothing apart from their poverty." If that is the measure, then world society must be judged as cruel and pitiless for its treatment of suffering humanity.

The heart's reason is more effective in presenting Jesus' dream than any learned doctrine, and it will make its principal herald, Francis of Rome, become a fascinating figure, reaching out to many Christian hearts and many others.

What Has Pope Francis Brought Us That Is New?

IT IS RISKY TO MAKE an assessment of the papacy of Francis because there has not been enough time to gain a vision of it as a whole. By a sort of blind reading, which only grasps the relevant points, we could make a list as follows:

1. *From church winter to church spring.* We are coming out of two papacies characterized by a return to strict discipline and control of doctrines. That strategy created a "winter" that froze many initiatives. Coming from the Third World, outside old European Christendom, Pope Francis has inspired hope, relief, and joy in living and studying the Christian faith. Once again the church has entered a spiritual "spring."

2. *From fortress to open house.* The two previous popes gave the impression that the church was a fortress, surrounded by enemies against whom we need to defend ourselves, especially against relativism, modernity, and postmodernity. Pope Francis has said clearly: "Anyone approaching the church must find open doors, not border guards of the faith. It is better that for the church to have an accident by going out in the street than that it should be sick and suffocated from staying indoors in the temple." So we must cultivate trust more than fear.

3. *From pope to bishop of Rome.* All the previous popes thought of themselves as popes of the universal

church, bearers of supreme power over all the other churches and the faithful. Francis prefers to call himself bishop of Rome, and thus he restores the oldest memory of the church. He refuses the title of Your Holiness, because, he says, we are all brothers and sisters. He has renounced all the titles of power and honor. The new papal ring, whose initial design was to have the pope's name and all his titles, now plainly says only *Francis, bishop of Rome.*

4. *From papal apartment to guesthouse. Francis* is more than just a name. It is an indicator of a different project for the church along the lines of Saint Francis of Assisi: a poor church for the poor, as he himself said, a church that is humble, simple, and smells of sheep, rather than of altar flowers. He wants and needs community. That is why he left the papal apartment in the Apostolic Palace and went to live in a guesthouse, a simple accommodation where he eats in community with the other guests. As he says: The papal apartment in the Apostolic Palace is not luxurious. It is old, tastefully decorated and large, but not luxurious. But in the end it is like an inverted funnel. It is big and spacious, but the entrance is really tight. People can come only in dribs and drabs, and I cannot live without people. I need to live my life with others" *(America)*.

5. *From doctrine to encounter.* He does not present himself as a doctor but as a pastor. He behaved in an intimately human way toward the African refugees on the island of Lampedusa. He denounced the money fetishism and the world financial system that martyrs whole countries. Thus he captures the chief insights of liberation theology, without calling it that by name. On June 17, 2013, at a Rome diocese convention, he said: "A Christian who is not a revolutionary today isn't a Christian"; we

must change hearts by sharing God's love. And he told a group of students that it is the duty of a Catholic to become involved in politics; "politics," he explained, "is one of the highest forms of charity because it seeks the common good." And he said to President Kirchner: "It is the first time we have had a Peronist pope." Indeed, he never conceals his support for the Peronist ideal of social justice. The previous popes placed politics under suspicion for fear of a possible ideologization of the faith.

6. *From exclusion to inclusion.* The previous popes, especially Benedict XVI, stressed the Catholic Church's exclusivity as Christ's only heir, outside of which there is a risk of damnation. Francis, bishop of Rome, prefers dialogue among the churches, including the other religions, in order to promote the building of world peace.

7. *From church to world.* The previous popes stressed the church, reinforcing its institutions and doctrines. For Pope Francis, the world, the poor, the protection of the earth, and care for life are the most important issues. The question is how the churches can help to safeguard the earth's vitality and the future of life.

8. *From the world to the poor.* In the first interview he gave to journalists, on March 16, 2013, Pope Francis called for "a poor church for the poor." He has put the poor at the center, visiting African refugees on the island of Lampedusa, other refugees at the Jesuit Refugee Center in Rome, and the unemployed in Corsica. He exemplifies a life of poverty by giving up any trappings of the rich of this world. He is bringing fresh air, new music, and new words for old problems, which make it possible for us to think that the church can look forward to a new "spring."

The Legacy of Pope Francis's Visit to Brazil

IT IS NOT EASY TO sum up in a few words the most important features of Pope Francis's visit to Brazil. I mention
some at the risk of leaving out other important ones.

The *main legacy* is the figure of Pope Francis: a *humble
servant* of the faith, stripped of all finery, touching and
allowing himself to be touched, speaking the language of
the young, and telling truths with sincerity. He represents
the most noble of leaders, the servant guide who does
not refer to himself but to others with affection and care,
rousing hope and trust in the future.

In the *political area* he found in Brazil a country rocked
by the many demonstrations by young people. He
defended their utopia and their right to be heard. He
presented a humanistic vision of politics and economics
and called for the eradication of poverty. He strongly
criticized a financial system that sidelines people at both
ends of life: older people because they do not produce,
and the young because there are no jobs for them. The
old cease to pass on their experience, and the young are
deprived of building the future. A society like that can
collapse.

A recurring theme was ethics founded on the transcendent dignity of the person. Referring to democracy,
he coined the expression *social humility*, which means
talking face to face, among equals, and not down "from
above." Between egoistic indifference and violent protest
he signaled an option that is always possible: constructive

dialogue. He stressed three categories constantly: dialogue as mediation for conflicts, closeness to people beyond all bureaucracy, and the culture of encounter. Everyone has something to give and something to receive. On July 27, 2013, in Rio de Janeiro, the pope stated clearly: "Today, either we stake all on dialogue, on the culture of encounter, or we all lose."

In the *religious area* he spoke out more fully and directly. He recognized that the "young have lost faith in the church and even in God because of the incoherence of Christians and gospel ministers." His harshest speech was for the Latin American bishops. He recognized that the church, including himself, is backward in the ways in which it is present in the world. He proclaimed not only the need to open the doors to all, but also to go out toward the world and the "existential peripheries." He criticized the princely psychology of members of the hierarchy, since they should be poor both inwardly and outwardly. Pastoral work should be founded on two mainstays: *closeness* to the people, over and above all concern about organization; and *encounter*, marked by affection and tenderness. He even spoke of a necessary "revolution of tenderness," which he personally displays in his life. He sees the church as a loving mother and believes pastors should develop this motherly attitude toward the faithful. The church must not be a controller and administrator but a servant and facilitator. He emphatically stated that the position of pastor is not in the center but at the periphery. He set the laity in the center to decide with their pastors on the way the community should go.

Regarding *dialogue with the modern world and religious diversity*, Pope Francis showed no fear of the modern world. He wants exchange and a deep sense of solidarity, a joining with those deprived of food and education. All religions must work together for the victims. It does not matter whether those paying attention are Christians,

Jews, Muslims, or anyone else. The important thing is that the poor should have access to food and education. No religion can sleep soundly while the disinherited of this world are calling for help. This is an ecumenism of mission, all working together in the service of others.

To the young he gave words of enthusiasm and hope. Against a culture of consumerism and dehumanization he called upon them to become revolutionaries and rebels. The future enters through the window of the young. He criticized the restorationism of some groups and the utopianism of others. He placed the emphasis on today: "Eternal life is at stake today." He dared the young to be enthusiastic and creative, to go about the world spreading the generous and humanitarian message of Jesus, the God who came close to us and went out to meet human beings.

In the final celebration in Brazil, there were more than three million people—happy, festive, and behaving in an orderly way. An air of warmth, peace, and happiness descended upon the city of Rio de Janeiro and all Brazil, which could only be the glow from the tender and affectionate Pope Francis and the divine feeling he managed to transmit.

Part III

The Reform of the Papacy by Francis

*Bishop of Rome and
Pope of the Universal Church*

Return to the Practice of Jesus Will Save the Church

Pope Francis is surely led by a dream because dreams are what always drive those who create new ways and bring in great changes.

The Dream of Francis of Assisi

What is Pope Francis's dream? I am sure that when he chose the name Francis he was inspired by the dream of Saint Francis of Assisi—to restore the church to the following of Jesus of Nazareth. For the sake of this dream Francis of Assisi, a rich young man, became poor, humble, full of tenderness and compassion, stripped of all power, close to all—the natural creatures whom he called brothers and sisters, but especially to those living in the worst of the "existential peripheries," the lepers.

This radically human Jesus, whose nativity scene Francis set up in the Greccio manger, spoke to Francis from the cross in the Church of San Damiano. This Jesus, whom he worshiped in the humble eucharistic species but above all embraced in the poor, whom he called "my Christs," was the one who directed all Francis's activity. Living the gospel "without glosses" (without commentary), the gospel pure and simple (following in Christ's footsteps), that was the dream of Francis of Assisi.

The Dream of Francis of Rome

The dream of Francis of Rome is no different. At the center stands Jesus, that poor prophet and workman who lived among us in poverty, simplicity, service, unconditional love, and unbounded compassion, close to all those around him, especially sinners.

God could be human like this man of Nazareth. Pope Francis believes that Jesus of Nazareth will save the church. It is not a wealth of doctrine or rigorous discipline that will regenerate the church but the practice of Jesus, that is, what the historical Jesus said and did. So, who fundamentally was Jesus?

Jesus taught us how to live as sons and daughters of God, as brothers and sisters to one another, in solidarity with the poor and oppressed, with moderation in the face of wealth, without discrimination against anyone, whether they are healthy or sick, sinner or saint, pagan or Jew, and as servants of every fellow human creature.

In the time of Saint Francis the church was in ruins because of the opulence of the popes and the worldliness of the bishops and the clergy in general. Today the church is also morally in ruins because of the sexual abuse and the Vatican Bank scandals. These grave failings have made the church lose its most precious capital: its credibility and morality.

Just as once Saint Francis of Assisi received a mission from the crucified Christ in San Damiano to reinvent another way of being church, so Francis of Rome was elected pope to rescue the freshness and attraction that the church has lost since it has become demoralized *in conspectu omnium* (before all the world).

This reformer had to come from abroad, from the periphery, far from the influences of the millennial ecclesiastical status quo. Pope Francis came from the South, not from any episcopal seat famous for its history. He is a son of colonial Christianity, which was always dependent on the great metropolitan and ecclesiastical centers. Over the course of five hundred years, this colonial Christianity has become rooted in our mestizo cultures; it has acquired a new face and engendered a surprising vitality and originality.

Francis of Rome comes from this cultural and ecclesiastical background. He has brought new features, which are the basis for his original way of being, acting, talking, and relating to people. Out of this originality he can project an institutional reinvention of the church and reconfigure the ancient structure of the Roman curia.

We must realize that European Christianity is in its twilight years, its death throes. Once it was a spring of living water. Today it is a pond of lifeless, stagnant water. It is beset with philosophical-theological, politico-religious disputes that have choked the freshness of the gospel. It remains trapped in the theoretical forms of Greco-Roman-Germanic culture. That culture produced its fruits; but fundamentally its time is now over. We need to free the power *(exousia)* of the figure of Jesus and the vitality of his message from a load that has become too heavy to be borne. It built up a superb cultural and theological synthesis in the Middle Ages. But that glory made the church so proud that it did not enter into dialogue with the new realities that were arising in history such as science, technology, nation states, democracies, modern freedoms, human rights, and rights of the poor.

So, it has become an increasingly closed and suffocating spiritual autarchy, with no capacity to renew itself internally or engage in cultural exchange with the surrounding culture. The church saw itself as a fortress, protected and isolated from the course of history.

That type of church does not have the right equipment to renew the institution and guarantee a meaningful future within the new planetary phase of humanity.

Renewal can come only from outside, beyond this heavy burden that was blocking any new initiatives. And it has come. That is the providential significance of Pope Francis. Let us look at some of his other characteristics that will have important consequences.

What Pope Francis Is Not

LET US TAKE A LOOK at some aspects of Pope Francis's personality and doings.

First, Pope Francis is not *Eurocentric*. He is not linked to those traditions that brand the Europe-centered church: the trauma of the Reformation, modern revolutions, and in particular, the way of living and thinking the Christian faith according to the logocentric paradigm of Mediterranean and Nordic cultures.

Pope Francis is not *ecclesiocentric*. He doesn't think of the church as being just about itself, setting itself up as the most important point of the Christian faith. He plays down the church "obsessed with doctrines and disciplines" and focuses on human beings in their questionings and quests, especially the poor, who are always made invisible and of no economic account. It is for them that the church should exist, "to warm hearts," to "walk with people at night," "to be with them as they are, with compassion" (interview, *Civiltà Cattolica*, August 2013; English translation, *America* [September 30, 2013]).

Pope Francis is not *Vatican-centric*. For him, the center is not the Vatican as a state, the only absolutist monarchy in the West. The first page of the *Annuario Pontifical,* which lists all the offices of the universal church with the names of the world's bishops and other institutions linked to the Holy See, does not give all the pope's titles. It simply reads, "Francis, bishop of Rome." He prefers to call himself bishop of Rome rather than pope. He harshly criticizes the careerism of curial officials; he considers their intrigues a plague and accuses them of having Vat-ican-centric mentalities, as if the Vatican were the whole church, above local bishops and national and continental conferences. He wants the curia to be an office of service and strength to the administration of the whole church.

Pope Francis is not *papal-centric*. For him, the church is first of all the people of God, not the figure of the pope. It was from the people of God that he first asked a blessing at his first appearance at the Vatican window as pope. Only after that did he give the papal blessing *urbi et orbi*. The pope takes over as bishop of Rome, calling the other cardinals and bishops his brothers. He has given up ev-erything that smacks of papal privilege: the papal throne, the golden ring, the pectoral cross encrusted with jewels, the shoulder cape—symbols of absolute power—as well as the precious chasubles and the red shoes. He has dis-missed this whole apparatus of power. He does not live in the papal apartment but at the Santa Marta guesthouse, as just one of the residents. He has also dismissed the security of the "popemobile" (the official limousine) and settled for an ordinary car, so that he can more easily reach out and be touched by the people. This befits the name Francis, as he is practicing the Poverello's ideals of simplicity and poverty.

Pope Francis is not a *restorationist* or *conservative.* To the amazement of the two previous popes, who were notori-ously sympathetic to traditionalists and even made major concessions to the reactionary followers of Lefebvre, he had the courage to say these harsh words in an August 2013 interview:

> If the Christian is a restorationist, a legalist, if he wants everything clear and safe, then he will find nothing. Tradition and memory of the past must help us to have the courage to open up new areas to God. Those who today always look for discipli-narian solutions, those who long for an exaggerated

doctrinal "security," those who stubbornly try to recover a past that no longer exists—they have a static and inward-directed view of things. In this way, faith becomes an ideology among other ideologies" *(America)*.

Representatives of Opus Dei, Comunione e Liberazione, the Legionaries of Christ, and other groups with their antiquated customs and observances are baffled and struck dumb. Pope Francis has a dynamic concept of revelation: "God manifests himself in time and is present in the processes of history. This gives priority to actions that give birth to new historical dynamics. And it requires patience, waiting" *(America)*. So, away with a church regarded as the repository of timeless truths! The times are pregnant with God. And God calls us through the signs of the times, a theme so dear to Vatican II, which Pope Francis has adopted in a pastoral attitude of openness and creativity.

Pope Francis does not see himself as a *master, doctor,* or *indoctrinator.* He has given up the sovereign role of being the only bearer of truth, unable to engage in dialogue or learn from others in whom the Spirit is also present. So he converses with a nonbeliever. He doesn't deny that there are absolute truths. But they only become manifest in a relationship of love and sympathy with others; they are not *un*related (*ab-solutus,* "disconnected"). That is why he has engaged in a surprising means of communication: not by official speeches, but ad hoc conversations, in which the sensitive heart's reason is more at work than intellectual reason. The effect is to give "flavor and perfume" to the gospel. He feels like a traveler (*homo viator*), along with other travelers in search of a fuller truth. That's what was said by Eugenio Scalfari, the former director of Rome's most important newspaper, *La Repubblica.*

Pope Francis does not see himself as a source of *certainties.* Traditionally, the certainty of faith was presented as a mark of its authenticity and truth. But a faith that is not rooted in history and does not run parallel to the way the world is running may just alienate people or be discarded as irrelevant. Anyone who keeps moving on the quest for God today has to endure uncertainties and doubts. The pope is not afraid to admit it:

> In this quest to seek and find God in all things there is still an area of uncertainty. There must be. If a person says that he met God with total certainty and is not touched by a margin of uncertainty, then this is not good. For me, this is an important key. If one has the answers to all the questions — that is the proof that God is not with him. It means that he is a false prophet using religion for himself. *(America)*

The pope's truth and humility here deposes all the institutional arrogance of a church that saw itself as the exclusive bearer of certainty, outside the daily lives of human beings and their ever-changing societies. So he stresses:

> God is always first and makes the first move. . . . We read it in the Prophets. God is encountered walking, along the path. . . . [This] is not relativism if it is understood in the biblical sense, that God is always a surprise, so you never know where and how you will find him. You are not setting the time and place of the encounter with him. You must, therefore, discern the encounter. Discernment is essential. *(America)*

Pope Francis does not see himself as an oracle but as a traveling companion who is not afraid of the most challenging frontiers. Faith's energy should go with us on the journey. He says: "Ours is not a 'lab faith,' but a 'journey faith,' a historical faith. God has revealed himself as history, not as a compendium of abstract truths.Our faith is a way, a historical faith. God has revealed himself as history, not as a compendium of abstract truths" *(America)*. Such a faith must pay attention to what is going on. So it always has to be renewed. As for himself, he recognizes: "Unfortunately, I studied philosophy from textbooks that came from decadent or largely bankrupt Thomism." But that should not be so.

What we are saying is unheard of in the pastoral and teaching practice of the popes. We are dealing with a pope who teaches by learning and who learns by teaching with humility and kindness. He shares in human lives, knowing that God has never forsaken anyone, however sinful and wrong. And he knows how to cry for human pain.

What Pope Francis Is

LET US CONTINUE WITH OUR attempt at a profile of Pope Francis. To get to know what he is and how he thinks, beyond his symbolic gestures and surprising words, three documents seem important. The first is the "Aparecida Document," produced by the Latin American and Caribbean Bishops Fifth General Conference, which took place in May 2007 in Aparecida, São Paulo. Its theme was "Disciples and missionaries of Jesus Christ, so that our people may have life in him." This document is important because it refers to Latin America and the Caribbean but always in the new context of the globalization of humanity, hence its universal value. Cardinal Bergoglio was its chief editor.

Normally the bishops conduct their discussions on the basis of a preparatory document. This time the document was not prepared in advance; it was threshed out directly from contributions and discussions in the assembly. Cardinal Bergoglio led the discussion, together with his Brazilian friend, Franciscan Cardinal Claudio Hummes, whose whisper in the pope's ear about remembering the poor inspired him to choose the name Francis.

Pope Francis himself finds this document so important that he personally handed it to President Cristina Kirchner of Argentina and President Dilma Rousseff of Brazil on the occasion of his enthronement to the Apostolic See, with this recommendation: if you want to know what I think, read this text.

In the speech he gave to the bishops from all Latin America and the Caribbean on International Youth Day in Rio de Janeiro in mid-June 2013, he confined himself mainly to a commentary on the "Aparecida Document." The document contains the main themes broached so far by the pope: the centrality of the historical Jesus, the poor and oppressed, encounter, closeness, and dialogue, the "revolution of tenderness," and the motherliness that should mark the relationship of pastors with the faithful.

The second document, a real guide to his pastoral work for the poor, is the speech he made to the African refugees coming to the island of Lampedusa in southern Italy. He denounced the culture of material wealth that leads us to "the globalization of indifference and our inability to cry" for the misfortune of our brothers and sisters.

The third document is the long interview he gave to the Jesuit journal *Civiltà Cattolica* in August 2013 (translated into English in *America* magazine). This resonated throughout every church and all round the world. In it he spoke freely of the centrality of Jesus, on faith that lives with uncertainty, and of a church that walks with the people to warm their hearts. He also criticized the hardliners and conservationists, the careerists and Vatican-centrics, the plague of the Roman curia. We list some points that suggest what Pope Francis is.

Pope Francis's *inspiration is the historical Jesus*: Jesus is the Son of God who became incarnate in our lowly human condition. Tradition has given him such magnificent titles that we can barely see him any longer as the preacher of the kingdom of God walking the stony paths of Palestine. What attracts Pope Francis of Rome, as it attracted Francis of Assisi, is the Jesus who preached a great hope for the people—the kingdom of God—and who taught us to call God *Abba*, dear Father, who had compassion for the hungry and satisfied their hunger, who saw Jairus's daughter dead and restored her to life, who wept over the death of his friend Lazarus and raised him to life again, who embraced children and raged against the Pharisees" ill will. Because of his practice and preaching this Jesus faced two trials, one religious and the other political, which resulted in his crucifixion. Inspired by Jesus, the pope says clearly: "The Church sometimes has locked itself up in small things, in small-minded rules. The most important thing is the first proclamation: Jesus Christ has saved you" (America). He saved us by teaching us how to live—not just by being pious adherents of a religious institution. Surely what the "Aparecida Document" states comes from him: "The church must fulfill its mission by following the footsteps of Jesus and adopting his attitudes" (no. 31). He continues: "Everything having to do with Christ has to do with the poor, and everything connected to the poor cries out for Jesus Christ" (no. 393).

Jesus is his perennial source of inspiration: in poverty, humility, tender love for the poor, compassion, and the will to reveal how God loves everyone, especially those who have strayed or are lost. It is impossible to imagine Jesus living in a palace, like Herod, or in the Vatican. His church would certainly never be built there. Rather, it is the Jesus of the Bethlehem cave, who bends over those who have fallen by the roadside and who multiplies loaves and fishes to satisfy a hungry crowd. That is why Pope Francis left the papal apartment and went to live where normal people live. He is following Saint Paul's advice:

> Let the same mind be in you that was in
> Christ Jesus,
> who, though he was in the form of God,
> did not regard equality with God
> as something to be exploited. (Phil 2:6)

For Pope Francis, this precept has become a way of life, first as the cardinal of Buenos Aires and now as the pope in Rome.

Pope Francis is *an advocate and defender of the poor*. This has been shown in almost all his speeches, as in the first speech he made to journalists, saying that he would like "a poor church for the poor," or in his homily on Lampedusa, or in Assisi in the Spoliazione hall of Saint Francis's stripping, or in his solemn speech about world hunger to the UN Food and Agriculture Organization. In accordance with the oldest episcopal tradition, in his case bishop of Rome, he always presents himself as advocate and defender of the poor. The face of the Latin American and Caribbean church, according to the "Aparecida Document," is marked by the preferential option for the poor, who have been excluded as Jesus was (no. 391ff.); this is always there in his words and actions. As the "Aparecida Document" beautifully puts it: "Only the closeness that makes us friends enables us to appreciate deeply the values of the poor today, their legitimate desires, and their own manner of living the faith. The option for the poor should lead us to friendship with the poor" (no. 398). This was his attitude when he visited the Varginha slum community *(favela)* in Rio de Janeiro.

He required the Latin American and Caribbean bishops to be "men who love inner and outer poverty, simplicity and austerity of life, men who do not have the psychology of princes." Indeed, in almost all parts of the Christian world bishops live in palaces, some sumptuous, as in Germany and Italy, as if they were Renaissance princes. Pope Francis's life of poverty and extreme moderation is an invitation and a challenge to all those in power in the church and to Christians, men and women, to imitate him and follow him because that was the lifestyle of the Nazarene. And it is a way of plainly showing solidarity with the poor and dispossessed all over the world.

Pope Francis sets the *world at the center*. Until recently, the major concern was to build up the church internally, free from the contamination of modernity, hence, the importance given to orthodox doctrine, discipline, strict observance of the liturgical rites, and clerical habits. A close watch was kept over doctrines and pastoral initiatives. That caused fear, desolation, and punishment, which robbed the church of its nature as a spiritual home.

In the face of widespread secularization, there was a new attempt to evangelize Europe in order to restore religious symbols to public life and regain lost cultural power. Vain initiative! Renewal does not come from externally visible, illusory techniques but from a new spiritual experience confronting and conversing in depth with the main trends of modern life. A wound cannot be healed by hiding it under bandages, but only by identifying what caused it and finding the appropriate remedy to make it better.

> The church's pastoral ministry cannot be obsessed with the transmission of a disjointed multitude of doctrines to be imposed insistently. . . . Proclamation in a missionary style focuses on the essentials, on the necessary things: this is also what fascinates and attracts more, what makes the heart burn, as it did for the disciples at Emmaus. *(America)*

Pope Francis comes from Latin America, a continent that for the most part did not undergo the crisis caused by the Enlightenment or suffer from the corrosive forces of the grand ideologies of material progress or from the two world wars. In Latin America a serene and, I would say, mystical faith lives on, because God and divine energies permeate the whole of life, even its most everyday events. That experience means Pope Francis does not share the distrust and fears of modernity harbored by his predecessors. He follows the spirit of Vatican II: first and foremost we must see the positive elements in all ideologies and historical movements. Then, by mutual dialogue, we can identify what is lacking on either side to help each other provide it.

We must not forget that the traditional church's proclamation of a God without the world enabled a world without God to arise. That is not the underlying theology of Pope Francis. With the eyes of a mystic he discerns the mysterious presence of God in all historical events and knows how to strengthen the light so that shadows do not darken hope.

The "Aparecida Document" clearly sets out Pope Francis's program:

> We need to go out to meet individuals, families, communities, and peoples to communicate to them, and share the gift of encounter with Christ, who has filled our lives with "meaning," truth and love, joy and hope! We cannot passively and calmly wait in our church buildings, but we must move out in all directions to proclaim that evil and death do not have the last word, that love is stronger, that we have been liberated and saved by the Lord's paschal victory in history. (no. 548)

As the document states earlier, "The church grows not by proselytizing but by attraction (no. 159), through the love and compassion that it openly demonstrates.

The church does not exist for itself but for the world it is called to serve. It is to be a humble sign that, despite the tribulations of current times, in the end all will be well, which is guaranteed by the resurrection of Jesus.

Pope Francis sees the church as *a field hospital:* he vividly describes the church's place and mission:

> I see clearly that . . . the thing the church needs most today is the ability to heal wounds and to warm the hearts of the faithful; it needs nearness, proximity. I see the church as a field hospital after battle. . . . It is useless to ask a seriously injured person if he has

high cholesterol and about the level of his blood sugars! You have to heal his wounds. Then we can talk about everything else. Heal the wounds, heal the wounds. . . . And you have to start from the ground up. *(America)*.

He has a dream deeply imbued with the gospel:

I dream of a church that is a mother and shepherd-ess. The church's ministers must be merciful, take responsibility for the people and accompany them like the good Samaritan, who washes, cleans and raises up his neighbor. This is pure Gospel. God is greater than sin. The structural and organizational reforms are secondary—that is, they come afterward. The first reform must be the attitude. The ministers of the Gospel must be people who can warm the hearts of the people, who walk through the dark night with them, who know how to dialogue and to descend themselves into their people's night, into the darkness, but without getting lost. The people of God want pastors, not clergy acting like bureaucrats or government officials. *(America)*

Pope Francis proclaims the *revolution of tenderness*. He asked the Latin American and Caribbean bishops for this revolution of tenderness in their relationship with the faithful, and this holds true universally. For him, the two fundamental things are closeness and meeting. This is the path followed by God when he decided to leave his transcendence and come to visit us. But as he said in a speech to the bishops of Rio, Francis recognizes that there are pastoral approaches that are "distant or disciplinary, focusing on principles, behavior, organizational procedures . . . clearly without closeness, tenderness, or affection." So he wants a church that is a spiritual home for the faithful, an open house for all: "Anyone approaching the church must find open doors, not border guards of the faith."

This attitude accords with what millions of Catholics long for. In the past they found ecclesiastical authorities who were keener on doctrines and ritual than pastors who "smell of sheep." Many who left the institutional church will now find reasons to return and take part, because they will feel welcomed and loved.

Pope Francis offers the virtues of the *good shepherd*. He cares for the faithful, walks with them, encourages them in hope, knocks and knocks, seeking closeness, meeting, tenderness, and compassion. No one should feel out of reach of divine grace. No one can be rejected by the church because of his or her moral situation, whether homosexual or divorced. For every fall there is a helping hand to get up again; for every sin there is forgiveness and compassion.

The virtues of Pope Francis are those of Jesus: love, kindness, acceptance, simplicity, closeness, compassion, and joy, feeling we are in the palm of God's hand.

Challenge for Pope Francis
to Embrace All Humanity

As a comment on an interview I gave to the newspaper *La Libre Belgique* on August 9, 2013, a reader (Marc den Doncker) wrote these words, which I consider worthy of reflection:

> The good Pope Francis frankly announces a revolution along the lines of a more fully human humanity. The pope says: "If anyone is a homosexual seeking God and is of good will, who am I to judge?" Perhaps in time the pope may express love for a homosexual person who is not seeking God, but who despite everything is a person of good will. That would be the influence of the Holy Spirit.

His comment continues:

> Perhaps in time the good Pope Francis may reflect in the depths of his heart on a poor woman who sticks a knitting needle up herself to get rid of a fetus conceived when she was raped, because she can't cope any more and feels in despair. And the good God, in his infinite goodness, may enable the good Pope Francis to understand the desperate situation of this woman, who is so distressed she wants to die. In his infinite goodness the good God may understand that a couple who decide not to have any more children should use the pill. And in his infinite goodness the

good God may make him realize that women have the same dignity and equality as men.

I am torn apart by the large number of tragic events that life brings us day after day. In the face of this real situation, is the church prepared to slide along a slippery road but in the direction of humanity assumed in full, driven by the Holy Spirit, who has nothing to do with principles and casuistry, which end up killing love for our neighbors? We must hope so.

Yes we will hope so, full of confidence.

Indeed, many ecclesiastical authorities, popes, cardinals, bishops, and priests, with some honorable exceptions, have largely lost the right sense of things; they have forgotten Jesus Christ's image of God, whom he addresses intimately as *Abba*, dear Father. That God of his showed motherly qualities toward the prodigal son, in seeking the coin lost in the house, in gathering us under her wings like a hen with her chicks. His main characteristics are unconditional love and limitless mercy: "For he makes his sun rise on the evil and on the good, and sends rain on the righteous and on the unrighteous" (Mt 5:45).

For Jesus, it is not enough to be good like the elder son, who remained in his father's house and obeyed all his orders. We must also be compassionate and merciful with those who fall or who get lost on the way. The only one Jesus criticized was this good son, who lacked any compassion and did not welcome his brother who was lost and then came home.

When he spoke to the bishops in Rio, Pope Francis recommended to them a "revolution of tenderness" and an unlimited capacity for understanding and mercy.

Certainly, many bishops and priests must be in a state of crisis when they are urged to confront this challenge. They have to alter radically the style of their relationship with the people: not bureaucratic and cold, but warm, simple, and full of affection.

This was the style of the good Pope John XXIII. There is a curious story that reveals how he understood the doctrines and the importance of meeting people cordially. What counts for more: love or law, dogmas or cordial meeting?

Giuseppe Alberigo, a layman of Bologna, extremely learned and committed to the renewal of the church, was one of the greatest historians of Vatican II. Prior to the opening of the council, he and a group of researchers published a critical edition of all the official doctrinal texts of the popes and councils since the beginnings of Christianity: the *Conciliorum Oecumenicorum Decreta*. Alberigo relates in the *Il Corriere di Bologna* that he was traveling proudly to Rome to make a solemn delivery of the weighty book to Pope John XXIII. The pope gently took hold of the book and sat down on the pontifical seat. Quietly he set the book on the floor and put both his feet on top of the volume (see Alberto Melloni, *Introducción al libro Ángelo Giuseppe Roncalli, Giovanni XXIII: Agende del Pontefice 1958–1963* [Bologna: Istituto per le Scienze Religiose, 1978], vii). It was a symbolic action. It is a good thing to have doctrines and dogmas, but doctrines and dogmas exist to support the faith, not to inhibit it or to serve as a means to categorize people or to condemn them.

It may well be that good Pope Francis will be moved to do something similar, especially with reference to canon law and other official texts of the magisterium that do little to help the faithful. First come faith, love, spiritual encounter, and the creation of hope for humanity, bewildered by so many disappointments and crises. Doctrines come later. Let us hope that the good God, in his infinite goodness, may lead Pope Francis in this direction with courage and simplicity.

The Tradition of Jesus and the Christian Religion

IN ORDER TO UNDERSTAND CHRISTIANITY properly it is necessary to make some distinctions; these are accepted by the majority of scholars. It is important to distinguish between the *historical Jesus* and the *Christ of faith*. By *historical Jesus* we mean the preacher and prophet of Nazareth who existed under Caesar Augustus and Herod. The *Christ of faith* is the content of the preaching of his disciples, who see him as Son of God and Savior.

Another important distinction that must be made is between the *kingdom of God* and the *church*. The *kingdom of God* is Jesus' original message. It means a complete revolution redefining the relationships between human beings and God (sons and daughters), with others (all brothers and sisters), with society (centrality of the poor), and with the universe (managing a new heaven and a new earth). The *church* became possible because Jesus was rejected, and so the kingdom did not happen. The church is a historical construction that tries to carry out Jesus' cause in different cultures and periods. Its dominant embodiment is in Western culture, but it has also been embodied in Eastern, Coptic, and other cultures.

Another important distinction is between the *tradition of Jesus* and the *Christian religion*. The *tradition of Jesus* comes before the compiling of the Gospels, even though it is contained in them. Thee Gospels were written between thirty and sixty years after Jesus' execution. During the intervening time communities and churches had been organized, with their tensions, internal conflicts, and forms of organization. The Gospels reflect and take sides within that situation. They do not claim to be historical books, but rather books for edification and spreading the life and message of Jesus as Savior of the world.

Within this tangle, what does the *tradition of Jesus* mean? It is that hard center, the content that fits in a nutshell and represents Jesus' original intention and practice (*ipsissima intentio et acta Jesu*) before the interpretations that were made of them. It can be summed up in the following points.

In the first place comes Jesus' dream of the *kingdom of God* as an absolute revolution of history and the universe, a contentious proposal because it was against Caesar's rule. Then comes Jesus' *personal experience of God,* which he passed on to his followers: God is a good Father (*Abba*) full of love and tenderness. His special characteristic is to be merciful and to "be kind to the ungrateful and the wicked" (Lk 6:35). Then Jesus preaches and lives by *unconditional love for others,* which he sets on the same level as love for God. Another point is that he puts the poor and invisible at the center. They are the first intended beneficiaries of the kingdom, not because they are morally superior, but because they are deprived of the basics of life, which leads the living God to opt for them. It is our behavior toward them that will decide whether we inherit salvation or not (Mt 25:44–46). Another important point is *community.* Jesus chose twelve to live with him. That number twelve is symbolic; it represents the community of the twelve tribes of Israel and the community of all peoples, who become the people of God. Last is the *use of power.* Only power that is service to the community is legitimate, and the holder of power must always seek the last place.

This set of values and visions is the tradition of Jesus. As can be seen, it is not about an institution, doctrine, or discipline. What Jesus wanted was to teach us how to live, not to create a new religion with pious faithful in an institution. The tradition of Jesus is *a noble dream*, a spiritual path that can take many forms and that can also have followers outside the religions and the church setup.

In the course of history the tradition of Jesus became a religion, the Christian religion—a religious organization in the form of different churches, especially the Roman Catholic Church. These had the character of institutions with doctrines, disciplines, ethical rules, ritual forms of celebration, and legal canons. In particular, the Roman Catholic Church was organized around the category of sacred power *(sacra potestas)* concentrated in the hands of a small elite, the hierarchy with the pope at its head, and excluding the laity and women. This elite makes the decisions and has a monopoly on the word of God. It is hierarchical and creates large inequalities. It identifies itself illegitimately with the tradition of Jesus.

This historical translation covered over much of the originality and delight of the tradition of Jesus with ashes. That is why all the churches are in crisis, because they became ends in themselves rather than ways toward Jesus and the tradition of Jesus.

Jesus himself had an inkling of this development when he warned that it was not much good keeping the laws and neglecting what is more important: "justice and mercy and faith. It is these you ought to have practiced without neglecting the others" (Mt 23:23).

And as for today: What is the attraction of the figure and speeches of Pope Francis? It is that he is closer to the tradition of Jesus than to the Christian religion. He says: "We have to find a new balance; otherwise even the moral edifice of the church is likely to fall like a house of cards, losing the freshness and fragrance of the Gospel. . . . The proclamation of the saving love of God comes before moral and religious imperatives" *(America)*.

There is no other way to regain the church's lost credibility than to return to the tradition of Jesus, as Pope Francis is wisely doing.

Pope Francis and the "De-paganization" of the Papacy

POPE FRANCIS'S INNOVATIONS IN HIS habits and speeches have caused a deep crisis among the conservative groups that strictly follow the directives of the previous popes. It was particularly intolerable to them that the pope received one of the initiators of the "condemned" liberation theology, Peruvian Gustavo Gutiérrez, in a private audience. They feel bewildered by the pope's sincerity in recognizing the mistakes made by the church and by himself, in denouncing the careerism of many prelates, in giving the name of "leprosy" to the sycophantic, toadying spirit shown by many in power, the so-called Vatican-centrics. What really scandalizes them is that he is turning things upside down, putting love first, along with mercy, tenderness, dialogue with modernity, and acceptance of people, including the divorced and homosexuals; doctrines and church disciplines come only after these things.

Voices from the more radical among them are already being heard making these sort of petitions: "For the good of the church" (their own good, obviously) and "Lord, enlighten him or eliminate him" (elimination of problematic popes is not a rarity in the long history of the papacy).

The most frequent criticisms circulating in the social networks of these historically antiquated and backward groups accuse the present pope of desacralizing, trivializing, and secularizing the figure of the papacy. In fact, they are ignorant of history and are still tied to a secular tradition that has little to do with the historical Jesus and

118

the lifestyle of the apostles. But it has a lot to do with the church copying the style of the pagan Roman emperors and the Renaissance princes.

The doors to this process were already open in the time of Constantine (274–337), who recognized Christianity, and of Theodosius (379–95), who made it the only officially recognized religion of the empire. With the decline of the Roman Empire, conditions were created for the bishops, especially the bishop of Rome, to assume functions of order and command. This occurred clearly with Pope Leo I, called "the Great" (440–61), who was proclaimed mayor of Rome to confront the invasion by the Huns. He was the first to use the name *pope*, which before then had been used only by the emperors. The tendency gathered strength with Pope Gregory I, also called "the Great" (590–604), who was also proclaimed mayor of Rome. It culminated later with Gregory VII (1073–85), who assumed absolute power in religious and secular matters, perhaps the greatest revolution in ecclesiology.

The current imperial, princely, and courtly vestments of cardinals and popes go back to Pope Sylvester (334–35). In his time a forgery was created, the "Donation of Constantine," that aimed to strengthen papal power. According to this document, Emperor Constantine gave the pope the city of Rome and the western part of the empire. The "Donation," which was unmasked as a forgery by Cardinal Nicholas of Cusa (1400–1460), included the use of the imperial insignia and vestments (the purple), the titles of pope and supreme pontiff, the golden crosier, the silk and ermine shoulder cape (mozzetta), the creation of the papal court, and residence in a palace. This is the origin of the present princely and courtly robes of the Roman curia, the hierarchy of the church, the cardinals, and especially, the pope. Its source is the style of the pagan Roman emperors and the sumptuosity of the Renaissance princes. So there has been a process of increasing worldliness of the church as a hierarchical institution.

Those who want to return to the ritual tradition surrounding the figure of the pope are not even aware of this historically closed and conditioned tradition. They are insisting on something that is inconsistent with gospel values and the practice of Jesus.

What is Pope Francis doing? He is restoring to the papacy and the whole hierarchy its proper style linked to the tradition of Jesus and the apostles. In fact, he is returning to the oldest tradition, "de-paganizing" the papacy in the spirit of the gospel, to which Francis of Assisi bore such emblematic witness.

The genuine tradition is on Pope Francis's side. The traditionalists are traditional*ist* but not traditional. They are closer to the palaces of Herod and Caesar Augustus than to the cave at Bethlehem and the carpenter's house at Nazareth. Against them stand the practice of Jesus and his sayings about renunciation, simplicity, humility, and power as service, and not being like the pagan princes and the great ones of the earth who subjugate and dominate. "But not so with you; rather the greatest among you must become like the youngest, and the leader like one who serves" (Lk 22:26).

Pope Francis is speaking out of this original tradition, which is the oldest, the tradition of Jesus and the apostles. So he is confounding the conservatives, who are left with no arguments.

With Pope Francis the Third World Has Entered the Vatican

THE MANY INNOVATIONS INTRODUCED BY Pope Francis are well known. He has made changes in the papal habits and in the style of presiding over the church, in tenderness, understanding, dialogue, and compassion. Many are bewildered because they were used to the classic style of the popes, forgetting that it is a style inherited from the pagan Roman emperors, from the name pope to the richly adorned shoulder cape, symbol of absolute imperial power, which Francis rapidly rejected.

We should remind ourselves once again that the present pope comes from the periphery, not the church's center in Europe. He has a different experience of the church, with different customs, and another way of feeling about the world with its contradictions. He deliberately expressed this in his long interview with the Jesuit journal *Civiltà Cattolica* (printed in English in *America* magazine): "The young Catholic churches, as they grow, develop a synthesis of faith, culture and life, and so it is a synthesis different from the one developed by the ancient churches." The latter are not marked by change but by stability, and it is difficult for them to incorporate new elements coming from modern secular, democratic culture.

Here Pope Francis stresses the difference. He is aware that he comes from another way of being church, developed in the Third World. The Third World is characterized by deep social injustices, by an absurd number of slums that surround nearly all the cities, by despised indigenous cultures, and by the legacy of slavery in those of African descent, who suffer grave discrimination. As well as its specifically religious mission, the church understands that it cannot evade an urgent social mission: to stand on the side of the weak and oppressed and struggle for their liberation. At various meetings, the bishops of Latin America and the Caribbean (CELAM) threshed out the preferential option for the poor—against their poverty and for the gospel of liberation.

Pope Francis comes from this church and cultural environment. Here these options with their theological reflections, with their own way of living the faith in networks of communities, and with celebrations that incorporate the grassroots style of praying to God are clearly in evidence. This is not the case for Christians of the old European Christianity, full of traditions, theologies, cathedrals, and a sense of the world impregnated with Greco-Roman-Germanic culture in its articulation of the Christian message. Because he comes from a church that puts the poor at its center, the pope's first visit was to the island of Lampedusa, then to the Jesuit Refugee Center in Rome, and then to the unemployed in Corsica. It is natural for him, but it is almost a scandal for the curia and without precedent for other European Christians. The option for the poor reiterated by the most recent popes was merely rhetorical and conceptual. There was no real encounter with the poor and what they suffer. For Francis, the proclamation is practical, warm, and effective.

Perhaps these words of Francis explain his way of living and seeing the church's mission:

> The church sometimes has locked itself up in small things, in small-minded rules. The most important thing is the first proclamation: Jesus Christ has saved you. And the ministers of the church must be ministers of mercy above all. . . . The structural and organizational reforms are secondary—that is,

they come afterward. The first reform must be the attitude.

So the center is not occupied by doctrine and discipline, which have been so dominant in recent times, but by the person of Jesus and human persons in their quests and in their seeking, whether they are believers or not, as Pope Francis showed in his dialogue with the former editor of the Roman daily *La Repubblica*, Eugenio Scalfari, a nonbeliever. New winds are blowing from the new peripheral churches, airing the whole church. Spring is arriving, full of promises.

Pope Francis and the
Political Economy of Exclusion

ANYONE LISTENING TO THE DIFFERENT speeches by the bishop of Rome, the present pope, feels at home. The pope is not Eurocentric or Roman-centric and certainly not Vatican-centric. He is a pastor who has come from the periphery of decadent and dying old European Christendom (only 24 percent of Catholics are Europeans). He comes from a new Christianity that has been working itself out for the last five hundred years in Latin America with its own characteristics and theology.

Pope Francis is not familiar with the central triumphant capitalism of Europe but with the peripheral subordinate capitalism that is a junior partner attached to great worldwide capitalism. Where he comes from, the great danger was never Marxism but the savagery of uncivilized capitalism. On our Latin American continent that type of capitalism has generated scandalous wealth accumulated by the few, at the cost of exclusion and poverty of the great majority of the people.

The way he speaks is explicit and direct without the mealy mouthed metaphors usual in the official, "balanced" Vatican way of speaking that stresses security and even-handedness more than truth and clarity in its own position.

Pope Francis's position starts from the poor who are excluded. That is completely clear: there can be no doubts or room to explain away this option since "there is an inseparable bond between our faith and the poor"

(*Evangelii Gaudium*, no. 48). In fierce denunciation he states plainly that "The socioeconomic system is unjust at its roots" (EG, no. 59). "We also have to say 'thou shalt not' to an economy of exclusion and inequality. Such an economy kills. . . . Human beings are themselves considered consumer goods to be used and then discarded. . . . The excluded are not the 'exploited' but the outcast, the 'leftovers'" (EG, no. 53).

It cannot be denied that such expressions by Pope Francis recall the magisterium of the Latin American bishops at Medellín (1968), Puebla (1979), and Aparecida (2007), as well as the common thinking of liberation theology, whose mainstay is the option for the poor.

There is a perceptible affinity with the economist Karl Polanyi, who was the first to denounce the "Great Transformation" (the title of his 1944 book) that made a market economy become a market society. Everything is for sale, even the most sacred and most vital things. Everything is for profit. Such a society is ruled by competition, by the prevalence of individualism, and by the absence of any limits. Therefore it respects nothing and creates a breeding ground for violence that is intrinsic to its structure and the way it functions. That was strongly criticized by Pope Francis (EG, no. 53). The effects have been appalling. He writes:

> To sustain a lifestyle which excludes others, or to sustain enthusiasm for that selfish ideal, a globalization of indifference has developed. Almost without being aware of it, we end up being incapable of feeling compassion at the outcry of the poor, weeping for other people's pain, and feeling a need to help them, as though all this were someone else's responsibility and not our own. (EG, no. 54)

In a word, we are living in a time of great inhumanity, heartlessness, and cruelty. Can we still think of ourselves as civilized if by civilization we mean the dehumanization of human beings? In fact, we are regressing to primitive forms of barbarism.

The pope concludes from this state of affairs that "we can no longer trust in the unseen forces and the invisible hand of the market" (EG, no. 204). That is how he attacks the false ideological heart of the dominant system.

And where does he look for alternatives? He does not drink from the social doctrine of the church. He respects it, but he notes: "We cannot help but be concrete . . . lest the great social principles remain mere generalities which challenge no one" (EG, no. 182). He looks to the humanitarian practice of the historical Jesus. He does not see this message as a rule stuck in the past but as an open inspiration in ever-changing history. Jesus is someone who teaches us how to live and live together, to "remain steadfast in our intention to respect others, to heal wounds, to build bridges, to strengthen relationships and to 'bear one another's burdens' (*Gal* 6:2)" (EG, no. 67). Personalizing his proposal he says:

> My words are not those of a foe or an opponent. I am interested only in helping those who are in thrall to an individualistic, indifferent and self-centered mentality to be freed from those unworthy chains and to attain a way of living and thinking which is more humane, noble and fruitful, and which will bring dignity to their presence on this earth. (EG, no. 208)

Pope Francis's dream is to make the historical Jesus' dream come true, the kingdom of justice, love, and peace. It was not Jesus' intention to create a new religion, but rather to form a people who love one another, live in solidarity with others, show pity, and feel all other human beings are their brothers and sisters because they are all sons and daughters of the Father in the Son.

This kind of Christianity does not proselytize. It wins people over by attracting them to its beauty and deep humanity. These are the values that will save humanity.

Dialogue Between Pope Francis and a Nonbeliever

FRANCIS, BISHOP OF ROME, PUBLISHED a letter in the newspaper *La Repubblica* replying to its ex-director, the widely known nonbeliever and intellectual Eugenio Scalfari. He had publicly put some questions to the bishop of Rome. Francis did something very important and unprecedented; he showed himself to be a man speaking to another man in a context of open dialogue, placing himself on the same level as his interlocutor.

Indeed, Francis replied to Eugenio Scalfari in a cordial way, with the warm intelligence of the heart rather than with the cold intelligence of doctrines. At present, in philosophy there is an attempt to restore the "feeling intelligence," which enriches and enlarges the "intellectual intelligence," because it speaks directly to the other from the depths. There is no hiding behind doctrines, dogmas, and institutions.

In this sense it is not relevant whether Scalfari confesses himself to be a believer or not, because each of us has our personal history and life story that have to be respected. What is relevant is the capacity of both to be open and listen to each other. To translate the words of the great Spanish poet Antonio Machado: "Your truth? No, the Truth. And come with me to seek it. Keep your own for yourself." More important than knowing is never to lose the power to learn. That is the meaning of dialogue.

With his letter Francis showed that we are all seeking a fuller and broader truth, a truth we do not yet have. Dogmas taken in themselves or doctrines formulated in the abstract are of no use in finding it. The general presupposition is that there are still answers to be sought, and everything is surrounded in mystery. This quest sets everyone on the same ground, believers and nonbelievers, and also the faithful belonging to the different churches. Everyone has the right to express his or her vision of things.

We all experience a terrible contradiction, which involves both believers and nonbelievers: Why does God allow the great injustices of this world? It is the question put with deep grief by Pope Benedict XVI when he visited the Auschwitz extermination camp. He laid aside for a moment his role of pope and spoke solemnly as a man with an open heart: "God, where were you when these atrocities happened? Why were you silent?"

Christians must admit that there is no answer; it remains an open question. The only comfort is the idea that God may be that which our reason does not grasp. The intellectual intelligence can only be silent because it does not have an answer for everything. Genesis, as the philosopher Ernst Bloch said, is not to be found at the beginning but at the end. Believers think that things are developing toward a happy outcome. Only at the end, in some way, will we be given to understand the meaning of existence. Only at the end will we be able to say "and everything is good." Only then will we be able to say a definitive "Amen." But while we live our lives, not everything is good.

Absolute truths and relative truths? I prefer to respond with the great poet, mystic, and pastor, Bishop Pedro Casaldáliga, deep in the Amazon: "The absolute? Only God and hunger."

I have great confidence that Francis with his dialogue will be able to do great things for the good of humanity.

He began by making an important reform of the papacy. Soon he will reform the Roman curia. Through various speeches he has signaled that everything is up for discussion, which not long ago would have been an unthinkable thing for a pope to say.

I believe that this pope is the first not to want a monarchical and absolutist government—"power," as Scalfari said. On the contrary, he wants to keep as close as possible to the gospel, which offers principles of mercy and compassion, with humanity as its central focus.

Certainly his dialogue with nonbelievers can truly broaden and open a new window to ethical modernity, which does not consider only technology, science, and politics, and can also lead to the overcoming of a behavior of exclusion typical of the Catholic Church, in other words, the arrogance of understanding itself to be the only true heir of the message of Jesus. It is always good to remember that God sent his Son to the world and not only to the baptized. He enlightens every person coming into this world, not just believers, as Saint John reminds us in the prologue to his Gospel.

In a letter to Pope Francis I have suggested an ecumenical council of the whole of Christianity, all the churches, including the presence of atheists, who through their wisdom and ethics can help to analyze the threats weighing on our planet and how to confront them. And first and foremost, women, generators of life, because life itself is being threatened.

Christianity presents itself as a Western phenomenon and now must find its place within a new phase of humanity, the planetary phase. Only thus will it belong to all and be for all.

In Francis, as he has already shown in Argentina, I do not see the will to conquer and proselytize, but, as he told Scalfari, the disposition to witness and to walk a stretch of the way together with others. Rather than an institution, Christianity is a movement, the movement of Jesus and the apostles. So the dimension of human dignity, ethics, and fundamental rights is more important than simply belonging to a church. This is the case of Eugenio Scalfari. It is important to look more to the light in history rather than the darkness, to live as brothers and sisters in the same common household, Mother Earth, respecting one another's options, under the great rainbow, symbol of the transcendence of human beings.

The church's long winter is over. Let us hope for a sunny spring, full of flowers and fruits, in which it is also worthwhile to be human in the Christian way.

Can the Roman Curia Be Reformed?

THE ROMAN CURIA IS MADE up of departments that help the pope in the government of the church, within 108 acres that surround the Basilica of Saint Peter. There are about four thousand officials. It started small in the twelfth century, but became a body of experts in 1588 under Pope Sixtus V, developed mainly to confront the reformers Luther, Calvin, and others. In 1967 Paul VI, and in 1998 John Paul II tried, without success, to reform it.

It is considered to be one of the most conservative government administrations in the world, and so powerful that it has managed in practice to hold up, file away, and annul the changes introduced by previous popes. It continues unscathed, as if it were working more for eternity than for time. Nevertheless, the moral and financial scandals within it have been so great that a cry has gone up from the whole church for reform. This is what the new Pope Francis has to carry out as one of his most urgent missions. As the premier Vatican scholar Giancarlo Zizola wrote (*Quale papa*, 1977):

> Four centuries of counter-reformation have almost wiped out the revolutionary chromosome of original Christianity; the church has established itself as a counter-revolutionary body and opponent of anything new that appears. In a speech to members of the curia on February 22, 1975, Pope Paul VI even accused them of assuming "an attitude of

superiority and pride toward the episcopal college and the people of God."

Combining Franciscan feeling with Jesuit rigor, will Pope Francis succeed in reforming the curia? Wisely, he has surrounded himself with eight experienced cardinals from all continents to help him carry out this Herculean task and the necessary purges that must be made.

Behind it all there lies a historical-theological problem that makes reforming the curia enormously difficult. It is expressed in two warring visions. The first one starts from the fact that after the proclamation of papal infallibility in 1870, with the consequent Romanization (uniformization) of the whole church, there was maximum concentration at the top of the pyramid: in the papacy as "supreme, full, and immediate power" (canon 331). This means that all decisions are concentrated in the pope, a burden that is practically impossible for one person to bear, even with absolute monarchical power. No decentralization is accepted, because it means a decrease in papal power. So the curia closes round the pope, making him a prisoner, sometimes blocking initiatives that are disagreeable to the traditional conservatism of the curial officials, or simply filing projects away until they are forgotten.

The second vision is aware of the weight on a monarchical papacy and tries to give life to the Synod of Bishops, the collegial organ created by the Second Vatican Council to help the pope in the government of the universal church. But under pressure from the curia, which saw the synod as a way of breaking the centralism of Roman power, Popes John Paul II and Benedict XVI transformed it into a consultative rather than a decision-making body. It meets every two or three years but without any real consequence for the church.

As Pope Francis has called together the eight cardinals to proceed with him and under his guidance to reform the curia, everything indicates that he will turn the synod into a body through which he wants to preside over the church. Let us hope that he broadens this collegial body with representatives not just of the hierarchy but of the whole people of God, including women, since they are the majority in the church. And this does not seem impossible.

As Pope Francis continues to ask us to pray for him, we must pray, and often, that his desire may become reality for the benefit of all.

Pope Francis and the Refoundation of the Church

POPE FRANCIS, LIKE FRANCIS OF Assisi, found a church morally and spiritually in ruins. In addition to sexual and financial scandals, it was involved in an internal power dispute within the Roman curia, to the point that Pope Benedict XVI was driven to resign.

The mission we see taking shape through Pope Francis's pronouncements makes plain that he plans to update Francis of Assisi's mission to restore the church. This requires radical structural reform, I would even say, a "refoundation" of the church, because the terms it uses go beyond reform, however far reaching. Francis is daring to refound the church on the basis of its original founders: the historical Jesus and the apostles. Theologically, that is well founded.

The current church model has now exhausted its historical and spiritual potential; it cannot find a way out (a favorite word of the pope's) of the institutional mess it has gotten into; it is incapable of addressing modern men and women. Pope Francis's proposal says: "Let's not be afraid to dream." In his words:

I dream of a "missionary option," that is, a missionary impulse capable of transforming everything, so that the Church's customs, ways of doing things, times and schedules, language and structures can be suitably channeled for the evangelization of today's world rather than for her self-preservation. (EG, no. 27)

He is aware that such an intention involves unavoidable ruptures. "We should not think, however, that the Gospel message must always be communicated by fixed formulations learned by heart or by specific words which express an absolutely invariable content" (EG, no. 129). "We cannot demand that peoples of every continent, in expressing their Christian faith, imitate modes of expression which European nations developed at a particular moment of their history, because the faith cannot be constricted to the limits of understanding and expression of any one culture" (EG, no. 118). "The ultimate aim should be that the Gospel, as preached in categories proper to each culture, will create a new synthesis with that particular culture "(EG, no. 129).

Such bold statements are only possible in the mouth of a pope who is no longer trapped in the antiquated schemata of European Christianity, which is in its twilight and a minority in the church worldwide. The language of that kind of church has lost its freshness, and its theology is becoming ever more repetitive and tedious.

The pope comes from another church background, less sedate, more colorful and flexible, which has appropriated the sounds and tones of its embodiment in the different cultures existing on the Latin American continent. It feels free to attempt a new church, which is up to the internal and external challenges, especially with regard to the devastating crisis in the life system and the ecosystem threatening the whole of humanity, and from which the church itself is not exempt.

In order to set about refounding the church, the pope is clearing the ground in advance in two areas: the politico-economic area and the ecclesiastical area.

What World Is the Pope Talking About?

Pope Francis speaks bluntly. He condemns the present economic-financial system as "unjust at its roots" (EG, no. 59). And he puts the poor right at the center: "There can be no room for doubt or for explanations which weaken so clear a message. Today and always, 'the poor are the privileged recipients of the Gospel'" (EG no. 48). He stresses this in these unconditional words: "No one must say that they cannot be close to the poor" (EG, no. 201).

Words like this when uttered by previous popes remained just words. They never met the poor with any effect or affection, hence, their difficulty in understanding a theology that made an option for the poor, against their poverty and in favor of social justice, which was the registered trade mark of liberation theology. However, this present pope goes out to meet the poor wherever they are, in Varginha in Rio de Janeiro, on the island of Lampedusa, in Corsica, in the horribly disfigured Vinicio Riva, who suffers from neurofibromatosis, which deforms the whole body. The pope embraced him for a long while, stroked his deformities, and gave him the experience of being a human being like all the rest of us. He attacks the ideological, perverted heart of the neoliberal economic system when he says: "We can no longer trust in the unseen forces and the invisible hand of the market" (EG, no. 204).

The pope's attitude toward the economy is one of prophetic denunciation. He accuses it in the harsh words of Saint John Chrysostom *(De Lazaro Concio)*: "Not to share one's wealth with the poor is to steal from them and to take away their livelihood. It is not our own goods which we hold, but theirs" (EG, no. 57). At the same time he adopts an ethical-political stance of standing beside the poor. One of the aims of preaching the gospel is "the inclusion of the poor in society" (EG, no. 17), which constitutes the key criterion of gospel authenticity (EG, no. 195). This sounds like the strong gospel expression of the Salvadoran liberation theologian Jon Sobrino: "No salvation outside the poor."

What Church Is the Pope Talking About?

POPE FRANCIS IS AWARE THAT the Roman-centric and Eurocentric church model has no way out. It no longer has the conditions necessary to recover the freshness of the gospel and the joy that the Christian message produces. It has caused what he calls "a desert" (EG, no. 86). The proposed refoundation is focused wholly on personal encounter with the historical Jesus, not idealized by later glorifying ideologies, but with the Jesus of the gospel, who became poor, simple, and humble. Jesus went about among the people giving us the gospel that we are children of God, together with unconditional love, compassion, and tenderness for the humble. Any renewal of the church must be imbued with that mission. But we have to understand the mission correctly. It is not a matter of winning people for the Christian religion, but of freeing people for others; we "remain steadfast in our intention to respect others, to heal wounds, to build bridges, to strengthen relationships and to 'bear one another's burdens' (*Gal* 6:2)" (EG, no. 67). The pope stresses that "it is not by proselytizing that the Church grows, but by attraction" (EG, no. 15).

These fundamental changes come under the name of pastoral conversion, which includes the papacy.

Pope Francis confronts the conservative and antiquated mentality of many Christians, harshly criticizing them. Such an attitude was unheard of in the papal magisterium of the last two centuries. Generally, it was the progressive groups who were watched, warned, interrogated, marginalized, and punished. Now "the Church, in her commitment to evangelization, appreciates and encourages the charism of theologians and their scholarly efforts to advance dialogue with the world of cultures and sciences" (EG, no. 133) and to help "the judgment of the Church to mature (*Dei Verbum*, no. 12, quoted in EG, no. 40).

Evangelii Gaudium is full of joy, hope, and innovative boldness. Francis wants a church that is home to all and for all, not a jungle of tangled doctrines. His position is founded on philosophical realism, according to which reality always goes beyond the idea of it or is superior to the idea. That principle of the primacy of reality prevents "ideas disconnected from realities [from giving] rise to ineffectual forms of idealism and nominalism, capable at most of classifying and defining, but certainly not calling to action." (EG, no. 232). That is what has mainly happened in the European church since the Protestant Reformation: the inflation of the doctrinal above the pastoral. The magisterium largely has lost its good sense because it simply closed inward upon itself, formulated the ideology of papal infallibility, became alienated from the course of history or directly opposed it. The most obvious pastoral and moral matters were put under suspicion, to the perplexity and scandal of the faithful.

Pope Francis is trying to rescue the obvious in life and translate the Christian message into language that all can understand. He accuses the church of "should-ism" (*habriaqueísmo*—a new coinage to mean entertaining ourselves by talking about what *should* be done but with nothing really being done).

He is especially hard on the spiritual worldliness of those Christians who claim to be preaching the gospel, especially on television, but are really preaching themselves and are more concerned with their own appearance in liturgical exhibitionism, in gaudy array, than with the gospel message. They are self-serving (see EG, no. 95).

This spontaneously brings to mind well-known media figures who are showmen rather than preachers of the gospel. Others have developed a "tomb psychology" that "slowly transforms Christians into mummies in a museum" (EG, no. 83). And then there are those who make the church become "a museum piece" or "the property of a select few" (EG, no. 95).

Humorously, he says there are gospel preachers who look like they have "just come back from a funeral" (EG, no. 10), who live in a permanent "Lent without Easter" (EG, no. 6). They are "querulous and disillusioned pessimists, sourpusses" (EG, no. 85) with the attitude of "defeated generals" (EG, no. 96).

What Pope Francis wants are Christians who are bold, resolute innovators who dare to get there first (*primerear*, a papal neologism), meaning those who are first to commit themselves (EG, no. 20). They are the ones who open a way out for the church. The term *way out* recurs throughout the exhortation. It points to a church that ceases to stick at home in its castle and goes out to dive into the complex, contradictory modern world, which is thirsting for meaning and the word. That is the meaning of "way out." Let us go out, out to offer the life of Jesus Christ to all!

> I prefer a Church which is bruised, hurting and dirty because it has been out on the streets, rather than a Church which is unhealthy from being confined and from clinging to its own security. I do not want a Church concerned with being at the center and which then ends by being caught up in a web of obsessions and procedures. (EG, no. 49)

Pope Francis envisages reforming the papacy and the Roman curia. He wants to decentralize institutional offices, give women decision-making powers, and set the people of God at the center. He wants to include laymen and laywomen fully in determining the ways the church should go. All these reforms will give the Catholic Church another face, open to ecumenical and interreligious dialogue.

Can We Speak of a Refoundation of the Church?

What I am about to say may well perplex Christians who have not had the opportunity to go deeply into theological questions. Most of them—and the catechisms are largely responsible for this narrowness—imagine that the church was born fully formed from the hands of Christ. Exegetical studies from more than two centuries ago have shown that, in fact, the formation of what we call the church was complex.

However, before we go into detail about this thorny question, we must correctly analyze this sentence, which only appears in Matthew 16:18. Jesus says: "And I tell you, you are Peter, and on this rock I will build my church, and the gates of Hades will not prevail against it." The context gives us the true meaning of the sentence:

> Jesus is testing the apostles' faith. "But who do you say that I am?" Simon Peter answered, "You are the Messiah, the Son of the living God." And Jesus answered him, "Blessed are you, Simon son of Jonah! For flesh and blood has not revealed this to you, but my Father in heaven. And I tell you, you are Peter . . . " (Mt 16:15–18).

But let us look carefully. What makes Simon become Peter is not Simon himself but his profession of faith. Jesus focuses on that. And on this faith in Jesus as Christ and Son of God, proffered for the first time by Simon Peter, the church will be built, yesterday, today, and forever. The important thing was not Simon but his faith. The following verses make that very clear when, instead of calling Peter "blessed," he says: "Get behind me, Satan! You are a stumbling block to me; for you are setting your mind not on divine things but on human things" (Mt 16:23). Even though Peter had confessed the faith correctly, he had misunderstood it. He imagined Jesus as a liberating political messiah and not the suffering messiah, who was going to "undergo great suffering at the hands of the elders and chief priests and scribes" (Mt 16:21). So the church is built on Peter's faith and the faith of all who come after him in the centuries to come. Without that faith there is no church. Therefore the most correct theological definition of church is the "community of those who have faith" *(communitas fidelium)*. That is the original meaning of this passage, and that is how it was understood in the early centuries. It was only later, in disputes about which church should have primacy, that the stress began to be placed on the person of Peter and not on what really counts, his faith. Wherever people gather together in this faith professed by Peter, there the church arises. Whether it is under a mango tree, in a peripheral community, or in a small group that becomes involved in faith in Jesus' cause, there will be the church and the presence of Christ. So, now that this point has been clarified, we can move forward in understanding a possible refoundation of the church.

For the church to arise three necessary conditions had to be fulfilled. The first one was the rejection and execution of Jesus on the cross, the result of which was that his central message, the kingdom, could not come about. The second one was the expectation by the apostles and the early Christians (see the first Epistle to the Thessalonians, dated 51/52, the first New Testament writing) that Jesus would return shortly in pomp and glory, which did not happen. Saint Luke understood well at the beginning of the Acts of the Apostles that Jesus is not the one who is coming but the one who went away, since he ascended into heaven. That left a space for something to arise that would take Jesus' message forward. The third condition was the decision taken by the apostles to found the church as an autonomous body, to "come out" and cease being a Jewish sect living with their goods in common in Jerusalem and frequenting the Temple to pray.

They met at the Council of Jerusalem and made a decision: "It has seemed good to the Holy Spirit and to us" to go to the Gentiles. They took elements of Jesus' message (his words, Eucharist, baptism, and the Twelve) and founded the actual church. In Pope Francis's language the church was born from this "going out" toward the Gentiles and the world. If they had not gone out like that, they would have continued to be a Jewish sect, confined to Palestine. So in its essential elements the church was pre-formed by Christ. But not only by him. There was also the apostles' necessary decision to take up the challenge of going out into the world, under the inspiration of the Holy Spirit, founding communities that continue up to our own days. Joseph Ratzinger, afterward Pope Benedict XVI, was the one who described well this process of church creation—the elements provided by Jesus and the apostles' decision—in his inspired book *O destino de Jesus e a Igreja: a Igreja em nossos dias* [The destiny of Jesus and the church: The church in our days] ([São Paulo: Paulinas, 1969], 9–29). In this book he wisely concludes that if the church actually arose from a decision taken by the apostles, enlightened by the Holy Spirit, it will go on living if Christians and people of faith in the risen Christ and in his Spirit continually renew that decision and embody the church in the new situations that occur. So the church is not a fully established great work, finalized once and for all. It always remains open to "going out" again in order to proclaim Jesus' liberating message in appropriate language to every people and in every time.

And isn't that just what Pope Francis is doing? He is prolonging the decision taken by the apostles at the Council of Jerusalem. Together with his eight cardinal

advisers, he is inaugurating a new "going out'; he is repeating that "it has seemed good to the Holy Spirit and
to us" to refound Christ's church for this new time of the
globalization of humanity.

That will surely be only the first step. Others will come
who will institutionally configure the church in other
ways, no longer Eurocentric, Vatican-centric, or papal-
centric, but Jesus centered, Spirit centered, people centered (centered on the notion of the people of God, as the
pope has said a number of times), and world centered.

There was a man sent by God to fulfill this messianic
mission. His name is Francis of Rome, inspired by Francis of Assisi. Both were called, each in his own time, to
restore and refound the church of Christ and the apostles.
This is now happening in a coherent and persistent way,
although of course there is opposition. We will have
another kind of church in the globalized world and not
just in one part of it, the West. It will be the Pentecost
church in which the peoples of the world are represented.
Pentecost was just the beginning. It continues and is still
happening today.

A Council of All Christianity?

As I WRITE THIS WE are celebrating the fiftieth anniversary of the death of John XXIII (d. 1963), perhaps the most important pope of the twentieth century. He is responsible for the renewal of the Catholic Church, which tried to define its place in the modern world.

On January 25, 1959, without telling anybody, he declared before the astonished cardinals gathered in the Benedictine Abbey of Saint Paul Outside the Walls, that he was calling an ecumenical council. Of his own accord he had made a critical judgment on the situation of the world and the church. He had seen that we were entering a new historical era, that of the modern world, with its science, technology, freedoms, and rights. The church should take a positive stance toward this emerging situation. Up till then its attitude had been one of mistrust and condemnation. The pope understood that such behavior drove the church into paralyzing isolation, which would be harmful to it.

Pope John repeated the old saying, *vox temporis vox Dei* (the voice of the time is the voice of God), and added, "This does not mean that the whole world, just as it is, represents the voice of God, but that everything carries a message from God, to follow if it is good and for us to change it if it is bad."

The Second Vatican Council took place in Rome (1962–65). The pope inaugurated it but died before it ended. However, his spirit marked that whole event with consequences still with us today.

He had two main watchwords: *aggiornamento* (updating) and *pastoral council*. *Aggiornamento* means saying yes to what is new, to bringing the church up to date in its language and way of presenting itself in the world. *Pastoral council* tried to express a relationship of openness, dialogue, welcome, and fellowship with people and the world. So, there were no condemnations of modernism and the new theology, when there had been such furious ones before. Instead of doctrines, mutual dialogue, mutual apprenticeship, and exchange. Perhaps John XXIII's spirit can be summed up in this statement:

The life of a Christian is not a collection of antiquities. It is not about visiting a museum or academy from the past. Of course, that can be useful, as it is useful to visit ancient monuments, but it is not sufficient. We live in order to progress, even if this means taking advantage of the practices and experiences of the past in order always to go further along the road that Our Lord shows us.

In fact, the council did set the church within the modern world, sharing in its vicissitudes and its victories.

The church in Latin America immediately saw that there existed not only the modern world, but also a sub-world, about which very little was said at the council.

At Medellín (1969) and Puebla (1979) the bishops of Latin America saw that in this sub-world, where poverty and oppression reigned, the church's mission had to be the promotion of social justice and liberation.

Fifty years have passed since that council. The world and the sub-world have changed a lot. New challenges have arisen: economic-financial globalization and consequent planetary awareness; the dissolution of the Soviet Union; new forms of social communication (the Internet and social networks, among others) that have unified the world; awareness of the limits of the earth; and the possibility that the human race will be exterminated, and with it, the planetary project of humanity.

The categories of Vatican II are not now the ones we need to face this new threatening reality. Everything points to the need for a new ecumenical council. But it is not a question of summoning only the bishops of the Catholic Church. With the dangers threatening us, this is a challenge for the whole of Christianity with all its churches. If we want to save the life of our planet, we need to take seriously the alliance, proposed by the great biologist Edward O. Wilson, among the churches, religions, and techno-science (see *The Creation: An Appeal to Save Life on Earth*, 2007). How can these religious forces contribute to our continuing future? The survival of life on earth is the necessary condition for everything else. Without it, all projects are canceled and everything loses its meaning. Christians must forget their differences and arguments and unite in this saving mission.

Pope Francis has the conditions necessary to summon all the expressions of Christianity, men and women, to be advised by people with special knowledge, including nonreligious people, to identify how we can work together with a new feeling of respect, veneration, and care for all ecosystems, with compassion, solidarity, shared moderation, and unlimited responsibility. For we are all interdependent.

By his way of being and thinking, Pope Francis has awakened the sensitive and spiritual heart's reason in all of us. With it, together with intellectual reason, we will protect, look after, and love this unique common household that is the universe God has given us. Only thus can we guarantee life and a future for humanity and for Christianity.

Conclusion

The Pope of the Church as a Spiritual Home

FOR SAINT BONAVENTURE, THEOLOGIAN AND Franciscan mystic, one of the Poor Man of Assisi's biographers, Francis is the morning person who kept the innocence of paradise, and so we can call him a man of another age. Today we could say that Saint Francis is someone offering a different paradigm of church and culture. This is a paradigm characterized by care, simplicity, poverty, fellowship with all natural creatures, shared moderation, and a great passion for the poor and all who suffer in this world.

It would be a culture of voluntary simplicity, shared moderation, kindness to all, not of accumulation but of sharing in solidarity, of respect and love for our sister Mother Earth and for human beings who are all brothers and sisters, feeling themselves to be sons and daughters of joy rather than slaves to necessity.

Francis overflowed with the joy of living and fascination for the beauty of creation. He was a man with a tender heart and was so cheerful that he gave the impression that he was already sharing in the gifts of the kingdom of God. In the *Divine Comedy*, Dante calls him the "Sun of Assisi," because of the radiance he beamed.

Francis wanted a church at the base, with the poor and the most invisible of all, the lepers, a church that renounced all power and ostentation. He realized that a church organized around power, even sacred power, ends up losing that power, because it is easy for it to ally with other power holders, relegating the poor to a lower place, hence, the importance of the preferential option for the poor against poverty and for the sake of justice and life. Being on the side of the poor and open to all, the church becomes the bearer of the historical Jesus, who was poor and who addressed his message first to them.

In his life Francis achieved a synthesis between the most demanding dreams and the humdrum of the day to day. He united the highest peaks with the deepest depths of the human condition. He became an archetype of full humanity. Because of this he does not belong either to the church or to the Franciscan order, but to humanity. He is God's gift who helps us love our life, just as it is, in its light and darkness, but called to be transfigured and limitlessly humanized, whenever it combines two passions: passion for God revealed in the poor Jesus Christ; and passion for human beings, especially for the poorest and most oppressed.

Pope Francis passed on something of this aura and this dream in his free, unadorned presence, tender and close to the people, especially the poor. He really wants a poor church, poor bishops, Christians who make their option for the poor and for social justice. He called upon the young to become rebels and revolutionaries, words we have never heard from the mouth of any pope in the past.

Amid fears for the critical situation of the earth, life, and humanity, Pope Francis gives us the conviction that whenever the sun rises, whenever the fields are covered with bright flowers, whenever hands are held out to hold others' hands, and whenever a new creature is born, it is a signal that God still believes in his creation and in each one of us.

As one who "loves all things that exist" (Wis 11:24), God will not allow our lives to be destroyed or our common household to be wrecked, so that it can no longer house us or generously give us everything we need. Pope Francis, we repeat, goes along with ideas related to the message of Jesus, of a kingdom of God comprising love, justice, compassion, and peace—good news for all.

Francis represents a new dawn of hope, a sign that a new spring can burst upon the church, with all its vitality and splendor. In this way it can regain credibility and will truly become a sacrament of liberation for so many who are crushed by countless oppressions. It was for them, first of all, that Jesus came into the world, gave his life, and wants his representative to strengthen them in faith and hope. Francis is making the church become a spiritual hearth again, where it is good to live together, struggle, and celebrate life with others in dialogue, in closeness, tenderness, and love.

Postscript

Message of Saint Francis
to Young People Today

DEAR YOUNG PEOPLE, my sisters and brothers:

Like you, I was young once. I am the son of Pedro Bernardone, a rich cloth merchant. I went with him to the famous fairs in the south of France and Holland. I learned French, I got to know the world a bit, especially the minstrels' music and the love songs of Provence.

My Festive Youth

My father, who was very rich, gave me all the benefits of wealth. I led a group of Bohemian lads, who loved to spend many hours of the night standing at street corners, singing delicious love poems, and listening to the troubadours who told stories of chivalry. There were noisy parties. Thus I spent a few merry years.

After a time I began to feel a great emptiness inside me. All that was good, but it did not satisfy me. To overcome the crisis, I decided to become a knight and do brave deeds in battles against the Moors, but halfway along the road I stopped short. I entered a monastery to pray and do penance, but then I realized that was not the right way for me either.

Call to Rebuild the Church in Ruins

Little by little a strange love for the poor began to grow in me along with a deep compassion for the lepers who lived in isolation outside the city. I remembered Jesus, who was also poor, and all that he suffered on the cross.

One day when I went into the small Church of Saint Damian, I stayed a long time contemplating the wounded face of the crucified Christ. Suddenly I thought I heard a voice coming from him: "Francis, go and restore my house because it is in ruins."

Those words sank deep into my heart; I couldn't forget them. With my own hands I began to rebuild a tiny old ruined church called Porciúncula. Afterward, thinking it over, I realized that that voice referred to the church of men and women, prelates, abbots and priests, including the pope himself. This church was a moral wreck. It was riddled by immorality and hunger for power and wealth; cardinals and popes built palaces and sumptuous churches. Jesus certainly didn't want all that for his followers.

Discovery of the Gospel and the Poor

I had to drink deeply at the true source for the rebuilding of the church: the Gospels and the following of Jesus who was poor. Nobody inspired or ordered me. God led me to the lepers, and I had enormous compassion for them. What I had previously thought of as bitter, now, through love and sympathy, became sweet. I went about the villages preaching Christ's words in ordinary language that everyone could understand. I saw in people's eyes that this is what they hoped for and wanted to hear.

All Creatures Are Brothers and Sisters

As I walked about, I was fascinated by the beauty of flowers, birdsong, water burbling in the streams. I moved worms off the dusty road so as not to tread on them. I understood that we had all been born from the heart of the Father of goodness. That is why we are brothers and sisters: Brother Fire, Sister Water, Brother Sun, and Sister Moon—including Brother Wolf of Gubbio.

Many of my former companions at parties and entertainments joined me. A dear friend, Clare of Assisi, left home and wanted to share our simple life. We began a movement of the poor. We did not take anything with us, except the ardor in our hearts and the joy of the Spirit. We worked in the fields and begged for alms. We wanted to follow in the footsteps of Christ, who was humble, poor, and a friend of the poor. And in the midst of doubts, Pope Innocent III approved our choice in 1209, allowing us to preach the gospel of Jesus everywhere.

After a few years we had become a multitude, to the point where we did not know how to house and encourage so many people. You know the rest of the story. I don't need to repeat it. Later, with the support of the pope at that time, the Order of Friars Minor was set up, with various branches, which have lasted until today.

Dear young people, beloved brothers and sisters, I had an experience that you, being young, have certainly had too and are having now: a circle of friends, parties, dances. So we have something in common. Allow me to enter your time and tell you what the Spirit of God inspires me to say.

Love and Take Care of Mother Earth

First of all, I beg you to love and take care of our sister Mother Earth. She is ill and feverish. For a long time we have been exploiting her. To replace what we take from her in one year, she needs a year and a half to recover. To you Brazilians, the earth has given perhaps what is her most precious heritage: the Amazon jungle, an abundance of fresh water, a huge range of living creatures, and great expanses of fertile land. Guard this inheritance for your children and for all humanity.

If we do not want to see great disasters that will affect all living things, we must urgently form a global alliance to take care of the earth and one another. We are running a big risk. But if we act with responsible solidarity and take care of everything that exists and lives, we can avert this tragedy. And we are going to do it.

Siding with the Poor and Oppressed

Many sons and daughters of Mother Earth, your brothers and sisters, are poor and suffer hunger. Many have been lifted out of poverty and can lead a more decent life than before. But even so, there are still many lying in the streets who are victims of disease, drugs, and homelessness. Be like the good Samaritan, who bent down and helped them to get up. Jesus goes on being crucified in the crucified of this world. We need to take him down from the cross and enable him to rise again.

Restoring the Laws of the Heart

There is something I need to say to you from the depths of my heart: we need to change *our minds and hearts.*

We need to *change our minds* in order to see reality with new eyes. Scholars tell us today that the earth is alive, not something dead and purposeless, a kind of store of limitless resource that we can use at will. Resources are limited. Fossil fuels like coal and oil, the fertility of soil and seeds are limited. We must administer these goods and services well, so that they will be sufficient for ourselves and future generations.

Astronauts seeing from the moon and from their spaceships have told us that the earth and humanity are inseparable. They form a single indivisible and complex entity. So we human beings are the part of the earth that feels, thinks, lives, and worships. We are Earth and from the earth, as the first pages of the Bible tell us, but we have a unique mission: to look after it and keep all natural goods. We are the guardians of the inheritance that God and the universe have entrusted to us, so that it will last and meet our needs and those of our children and grandchildren.

As well as a change of mind, we need a *change of heart.* The heart is the seat of deep feeling, warm affection, and sincere love. The heart is the place where values grow. We need to restore the heart's laws.

As well as the intellectual reason that you use so much at school, at work, and in leading your lives, there is the heart's sensitive intelligence. Without it, with intellectual reason alone, we cannot hear the cry of the poor, of the earth, of the forests and waters. Without the heart's reason we will not be able to go out to meet those who cry and suffer, help them, give them our shoulder to lean on, save them.

So, my dear young people, you who are naturally aware of great dreams and the eagle's upward flight, you should always cultivate a feeling heart, a kind heart that is not ashamed to weep for the deep suffering of many of our brothers and sisters.

Learn to Live on Earth in a Different Way

I should like to tell you something else with confidence. It is important to begin a new way of inhabiting the earth. We cannot go on as we are. Up till now we have lived by dominating it with a clenched fist and subjecting everything to our own interests. We dreamed of unlimited progress. Today we are aware that the little, limited Earth cannot support a limitless project. We have reached its limits. And because we go on pushing at them, the earth responds with hurricanes, floods, droughts, earthquakes, and tsunamis. We must change if we want to survive.

Instead of a clenched fist, we need an open hand to give the care that is needed; we need to intertwine our fingers in a union of values and principles capable of supporting a new attempt at civilization. And at its center will be the life of nature, human life, and the life of the earth. Economics and politics will be more in the service of life than of the market and profit.

Change Begins with You

Dear young people, you must be the change that we want for others. You must begin living in the new way, respecting everything in nature, every plant, every animal, every landscape, because these have an intrinsic value in themselves, independent of the rational use we make of them. They are our brothers and sisters. With them we can establish a fellowship of respect, reciprocity, and mutual aid, so that we can all go on living on this planet, even the most vulnerable among us, to whom we will give more care and love.

Dear young brothers and sisters, resist the culture of accumulation and consumerism. Think of other brothers and sisters, the millions and millions who live and sleep with hunger and thirst and suffer greatly. Think every day and be concerned about the poor and their dramatic destiny, especially that of innocent creatures.

Consume with solidarity. Make those three "R"s real: reduce, reuse, and recycle. And I would add one more "R": reforest. Plant trees and restore deforested areas. Trees trap polluting gases; they give us shade, flowers, and fruits. Realize that less can be more and that happiness does not come from getting rich or from a profitable profession, but from sharing and behavior that is always human toward our fellow human beings.

Keep the Sacred Flame Burning Within You

Finally, dear young people, my dear brothers and sisters, none of this will work unless God is present in all our doings. He is nowhere in particular because he is everywhere. Above all, he is in your hearts. Within each of you burns a living fire and a sacred flame. It is the mysterious and loving presence of God. He can be felt most in the phenomenon of enthusiasm, which is so strong at your age. The word *enthusiasm* means having God inside you. This is the inner God, the God who is a comrade and friend, the God of unconditional love.

Our materialist and consumeristic culture has doused this fire with ashes and threatens to extinguish the sacred flame. Rake off these ashes by opening your hearts to God, keep a moment each day to think about him and talk with him, complain and weep before him, and ask him for something. Or do not say anything. Just stand in silence before God. He will speak to you and arouse good feelings and luminous insights. Never forsake God, because he does not forsake you and never will. Live as if he holds you in the palm of his hand. Then you will be protected because he is the good shepherd who will lead you into green pastures where you will lack nothing. He is Father and Mother of infinite tenderness.

God Is the Sovereign Lover of Life and Our Great Ally

As God took on our humanity in Jesus, he also took on a part of the earth and the elements of the universe. So these have already become divine and eternal. They will never be the target of threats, even though we ourselves can be. God always loves what he has made. He does not forget any creature born from his heart. So let us trust that he will protect our dear Mother Earth and guarantee the future of life, which is the future of all of you.

Don't waste time; it is pressing. At this stage we cannot be too late or make mistakes, because we risk losing any opportunity or way to correct these mistakes. But do not lose your enthusiasm or the joy of your hearts. Life always triumphs because God is alive and sent us Jesus, who said he had come to bring life and life in abundance.

That is all I wanted to say to you from the depths of my heart.

Finally, I ask you something very special: pray, support, and work with the pope who bears my name, Francis. He will restore the church today, as I tried to restore the church in my own time. Without your help he will feel weak and run into grave difficulties. But with your enthusiasm and support, and that of your groups and movements, he will accomplish the mission with which Jesus has entrusted him, to give our church a kind face and to strengthen everybody in faith and hope. With you, he will be strong and attain his ends.

Now, before we say goodbye, I give you the blessing that I once gave to my close friend Friar León, God's little sheep:

> May God bless you and keep you.
> May he show his face and have compas-
>   sion on you.
> May he turn his face toward you and give
>   you peace.
> May God bless you.

Peace and goodwill

Francis,
Your poor brother of Assisi